A FORGOTTEN HERITAGE?

STARTLING EVIDENCE THAT THIS UNIVERSE IN WHICH WE LIVE IS BUT ONE AMONG MANY OTHER UNIVERSES INHABITED BY MEN WHO ARE REAL AND TANGIBLE AS OURSELVES IN THEIR OWN FRAME OF REFERENCE.

BRINSLEY LE POER TRENCH, the author of THE SKY PEOPLE and the former editor of FLYING SAUCER REVIEW, has probably been aware of more well-authenticated flying-saucer reports than any other person in the world with the exception, possibly, of military intelligence departments.

"This is one of the most fascinating books that I have had the pleasure of reading for a long time—in fact, once I had started (TEMPLE OF THE STARS) it was difficult to put down . . . he must have gone to tremendous trouble in his research for data and you will be pleased to know it is well illustrated and indexed."

—THE ATLANTEAN

"This book opens a hundred gateways to the stars. Clues to the people who came from the sky and to the effects of their work abound in a strange profusion, but the pattern does not become evident until you adopt the right approach and start to ask the right questions."

—FATE MAGAZINE

Also by
BRINSLEY LE POER TRENCH

The Sky People

Forgotten Heritage

TEMPLE
OF THE STARS

formerly titled
Men Among Mankind

Brinsley Le Poer Trench

BALLANTINE BOOKS • NEW YORK

To Both Sides of the Street

© Brinsley le Poer Trench, London 1962

First published by Neville Spearman Limited in 1962 under the title *Men Among Mankind*

All rights reserved under Pan-American and International Copyright Conventions.

SBN 345-23832-X-150

This edition published by arrangement with Fontana/Collins

First Printing: March, 1974

Printed in the United States of America

BALLANTINE BOOKS
A division of Random House, Inc.
201 East 50th Street, New York, N.Y. 10022

Contents

Illustrations

Acknowledgments

I wish to thank John Maltwood for his kind permission to quote from the late Mrs K. E. Maltwood's book, *A Guide to Glastonbury's Temple of the Stars.*

My grateful thanks go to the Misses Mary and Agnes Kouroussidis for their researches into biblical history, and to Baroness Pauline von Taussig for valuable astrological notes.

The quotations at the heads of chapters are taken from *Lost Horizon* by James Hilton, published by Macmillan and Co Ltd, London, and reproduced by courtesy of John Farquharson Ltd, London. (Copyright 1933, 1936, by James Hilton.)

The photographs are reproduced by permission of the following: *Plates 2, 3* and *6*, Crown Copyright; reproduced with the permission of the Controller of Her Majesty's Stationery Office; *Plates 4 and 5*, Ashmolean Museum; *Plate 7*, French Government Tourist Office; *Plates 8 and 9*, Egyptian State Tourist Administration; *Plate 10*, Middle East Airlines; *Plate 11*, SS Grace Line.

'He that knows all things can do all things.
One has but to know – and there shall be wings.'
Leonardo da Vinci

Preface

Many people have had various ideas about the Great Pyramid at Giza, Stonehenge on Salisbury Plain, and that remote, mysterious island called Easter after the day upon which it was discovered by European Man. A goodly number of these people have written books. Impressed with the implications of it all, they have put pen to paper on such subjects as the lost continent of Atlantis, the Arthurian Legends and the fabulous story of Gilgamesh. Hundreds of biographies have been printed giving in great detail the lives of outstanding men and women: Alexander the Great, Leonardo da Vinci, the first Queen Elizabeth – all have been presented to the public more than once.

In this presumptuous book, the same thing has been attempted in a different way. There is a connection between such widely separated accomplishments as the Great Pyramid and Stonehenge. Through all the megalithic ruins around the world there runs a thin thread of forgotten history that weaves them all together into a pattern that can still be followed in the lives of remarkable men and women. It is an intricate design conceived in the dim, reed-bordered mists of Egyptian antiquity, and it goes forward with our history until we find ourselves being asked to fight for its principles in the name of our own Atomic Future.

Nearly any day now we can read in our newspapers of some new archaeological discovery. A few years ago there were the Dead Sea Scrolls. Then came the discovery of towns in Egypt that were flourishing before the two great kingdoms of the Nile were united. Lost cities have turned up in South America. Discoveries such as these have changed what was previously legend into sober, historical fact. Almost any professional archaeologist today can, with a little luck, become another Schliemann and unearth his Troy.

In Somerset, in the West of England, there is an amazing example of prehistoric earthworks. It has been called the

Temple of the Stars, and it occupies an area ten miles in diameter. Its hills and artificial waterways depict the signs of the zodiac, and if it can ever be properly investigated by trained and competent researchers, it may well prove to be our latest and most astounding example of a legend turning into historical fact.

This enormous monument consists of mountainous giants of the zodiac. An enormous planetarium, it reproduces on a grand scale a map of the heavens that only ages of geological upheaval could possibly destroy, and it bears within the elements of its design surprising evidence that it is older than the Pyramid.

It was at first thought that the rediscovery in modern times of this most ancient testimonial of Man belonged entirely to Mrs K. E. Maltwood, who in our own age traced the figures on the ground and arranged to have them photographed from the air, from which angle they are even more apparent and convincing. With sincere gratitude and without apology considerable space has been devoted in this book to the Somerset Zodiac and some of its possible significance.

The original discoverer of the Somerset Zodiac was the famous Elizabethan scholar, Dr John Dee (1527-1608). In John Michell's fascinating book, *The View over Atlantis*, there appears this passage.[1]*

'Mrs Maltwood, although she never knew it, was not the first to recognize the zodiacal giants of Somerset. In about 1580 the famous scholar and magician, Dr Dee, discovered what he believed to be Merlin's secret in the Glastonbury plains. According to his recent biographer, Richard Deacon, he became interested in "the unusual arrangement of the prehistoric earthworks in the Glastonbury area and had diagnosed that these objects when carefully mapped represented the signs of the Zodiac and the stars". He himself had made a map of the district on which he had noted that "the starres which agree with their reproductions on the ground do lye onlie on the celestial path of the Sonne, moon and planets, with the notable exception of Orion and Hercules . . . all the greater starres of Sagittarius fall in the hinde quarters of the

* The numerals in the text refer to the Reference Notes at the end of the book.

horse, while Altair, Tarazed and Alschain from Aquilla do fall on its cheste. . . . thus is astrologie and astronomie care-fullie and exactley married and measured in a scientific re-construction of the heavens which shews that the ancients understode all which today the lerned know to be factes." '

There are other mysterious places in the world, but, for European Man and his descendants, there are only three or four which hold perennial and continuing interest. We do not pretend to have discovered the ultimate reason for this un-dying fascination. We have noticed, along with many other people who have gone before us and others who are with us here and now, a certain connection indicated by all these monuments, without exception.

Between mankind on earth and another breed of man who is invariably credited with maintaining his abode among the stars, there is an ancient and traditional link, a brotherhood that reaches the epitome of its dramatisation in the legends of the Twins – a theme that runs through the basic mythology of almost every nation in the world, quite literally from the beginning of their recorded time. In our own scientific age it survives as an unquenchable popular belief in the influence of the stars. No amount of nuclear research will ever destroy the age-old acceptances of astrology. If the ultimate nuclear destruction occurred tomorrow, it would not be any one of the physicists who would be able to reassure the fleeing people. Much more probably it would be some competent and informed astrologer who could set himself up by the wayside, and with the help of his pack of *Tarot* cards, interpret the catastrophic conditions as they applied to each suffering refugee who might stop to ask him for comfort or for guid-ance.

This would be a terrible blow and a great indignity to Modern Science, but it would be an equally great and living testimonial to the age-old tradition of survival at the bottom of the pyramid. Among what is so contemptuously called the masses of humanity in our time, only the most fundamental of concepts has any possible chance of survival. The last Keystone which alone can tie the Arch will be found cast away among what is currently considered to be the rubble.

The possibly unusual datings to be found in this book have,

admittedly, been taken from a part of contemporary knowledge that is, at the moment, officially classified as rubble. We are not at all dismayed. On the contrary, because our stone does not fit well with the measurements required by most of the overseers, we are pleased with it. We do not contend that it has any proper place in the building as it may be conceived by anybody in charge of superintending the work at the present time. Nevertheless, we have it in hand, and we believe it may be useful, even though it fails to measure up to certain preconceptions currently accepted and taught by people in authority.

The point at which the sun rises at the Vernal (or Autumnal) equinox appears to move backwards through the zodiacal circle from year to year. This apparent motion of the sun against the fixed stars is called precession, and it produces the longest cycle given any prominence in astrological calculations outside the Hindu system, which combines complete precessions into longer Ages.

Calculations made at different times give different values for this Grand Cycle. The time-value built into the Great Pyramid amounts to 25,826.54 years, according to Dr Davidson and H. Aldersmith.[2] Rightly used, this value will give a long series of interesting results.

Geological and archaeological research have determined that about 4000 BC, and for some time before and after that date, great catastrophes occurred. Drastic changes took place on the surface of our Earth. The Alps and the Himalayas, the Rocky Mountains in North America, and the Andes in South America, were all considerably elevated at about this time. Part of the same upheaval laid down the deep stratum of alluvial clay still ten feet thick over the remains of Ur of the Chaldees.[3] Some 400 miles to the northward in the vicinity of Mount Ararat the ocean-contaminated deposit is still eighteen inches deep after having been compressed for thousands of years.

Some time after these geological disturbances had settled down, the zodiac was revised. There was a very real need for this revision. The year recognised by more ancient systems and incorporated in the legends that have survived to us from those times, and in the Gate of the Sun at Tiahuanaco, was much shorter. When the zodiac was redetermined after 4000 BC, it was corrected to a longer year of 360 days. Since that time the year has become still longer.

The natural conceit of later students of Astronomy and Astrology has led to the lodging of a charge of inaccuracy against the ancient observers. This accusation is belied by their obvious abilities in other fields of scientific accomplishment. There can be no real reason, beyond what may be dictated by self-esteem, to suppose that the old astronomers were careless in their observations of the positions of the equinoctial points and of the solstices. The very life of their communities depended upon an accurate calendar, by means of which the various operations of the agricultural year could be regulated. It is no more than human logic that great care would have been exercised in the production of such a calendar.

The entire system of Babylonian (Chaldean) mathematics was based upon the year of 360 days, the twelve signs of the zodiac, and the relationship between the diameter and the circumference of the circle. All this was borrowed later on by the Kabbalists and incorporated in their symbolic language of numbers. This is made abundantly clear by even the most superficial examination of the first chapters of Genesis from a mathematical point of view.

The oldest zodiac about which we can deduce any certain knowledge is the one upon which the Temple of the Stars in Somerset, in the West of England, was framed. This zodiac consisted of ten signs, unequally divided. Either this was a strictly interpretational zodiac, or it reflects some previous eccentricity in the orbit of the Earth during the catastrophic era marking the last few thousand years of the Atlantean period. Perhaps it was a little bit of both.

Since, at the time of the Great Revision, the year consisted of 360 days, we still divide our circles into 360 degrees. Any recurring cycle can be represented by a circle. Thus, the division of 25,826.54, the number of years in a Grand Cycle of Precession (according to Pyramid values), by 360 gives the value of each degree in terms of years. This value amounts to almost exactly seventy-two years, in round numbers.

The five-pointed star has long been used as a symbol of Man, particularly of perfected Man. There are many interpretive explanations of this symbol. Some of them are excellent in their conception, while others go wide of the mark and become shrouded in veils of mystical allusion, significant only to their individual inventors. As is usual in such cases, there is a simple, fundamental, and this time mathematical fact at the basis of it all. It involves the number 72 – that round number expressive of the number of years in one degree of the Grand Cycle of Precession. It represents the esoteric side of that number referred to in the Bible as the years of a man's life: three score and ten, the 72 having been rounded off to 70 in full agreement with good Kabbalistic discourse.

Divide 360 by the number of fingers on a man's hand – 5 – or multiply 72 by 5. Either way, the result is 360, to 72, to 360 – back and forth. In certain usages there is a reference to three, five and seven steps, which, illuminated by this process, reveals more of the details of the winding stair by which mankind must climb.

The hand and its *finger joints* were important to the Chaldeans and Babylonians in their manner of counting. The possible positions of the opposable thumb against the parts of the four fingers, each finger having its own three dimensions (joints), made esoteric sense on a cosmic scale, and appealed to those who recognised it as an ideal basis for numeration. This was the same system as that used by the Druids, and it survives today in British money and measure. It was realised that the principal external feature of mankind's anatomy that made him 'different from all other animals' was the hand. With it mankind is capable of doing many things no other animal can do.

Seventy-two, then, is the number of degrees between the points of a pentagram inscribed upon a circle. A circle consists of a single line. The five-pointed star, although it is a fairly complex figure, can be drawn without lifting the pen from the paper. This establishes its direct symbolic affinity with the circle, and it was this relationship that was taken as being representative of Man's relationship to his Creator. The unbroken circle has always been a symbol of the Supreme Being in manifestation – the sum total of Creation.

The new revised zodiac consists of twelve signs. The revisers had very orderly and systematic minds, and, in addition, it is not at all unlikely that the real reasons for the older, unequal division of the zodiacal circle had either been lost during the long period of terrestrial upheavals, or they had actually disappeared. At any rate, it was possible to divide the year into twelve equal portions, and this is exactly what the reformers did. Each sign now has thirty degrees allotted to it. In terms of years in the Grand Cycle of Precession, this amounts, in round numbers, to 2152 years. Thus, 2152 years is the length, or period, of each successive Astrological Age within the precessional cycle. Each one of these Ages can be called a Month in the Great Zodiacal year, and each of the thirty days of such a Month amounts to approximately seventy-two years.

The Great Month is reflected in the story of the life of Jesus. He was said to be thirty years old when he reached his spiritual maturity, came to John at the River Jordan to be baptised, and began his ministry. This has been taken to mean that his message applied directly and specifically to one Zodiacal Age – the Age of Pisces, which is a Water Sign – the age which was just beginning when he was born. The jump from the exoteric to the esoteric meaning of water, the transition from the Ages of the Fishes to the Age of the Water-bearer, is one of the reasons his second coming is so widely expected at this time. The world has entered upon the next precessional period – the Month of the Sign of Aquarius. Here again there is much misinterpretation and confusion to be sorted out and reconsidered, as more data is released to the world.

1. Hewers of Stone

It is an intricate story, if you would care to hear it.
— *The High Lama*

On 30 September, 1940, Time, the weekly news magazine, printed an interesting story.

5,000-year Journey

Two years ago the publicity men of Westinghouse Electric & Manufacturing Co., who are proud of 20th century civilisation, decided to leave a memento of their civilisation to the future. The memento was not just a written record, but a miniature museum, an assortment of characteristically 20th century objects packed into a 'Time Capsule'. It just happened that the New York World's Fair was coming up, so they decided to address the capsule to savants of 6939 — 5,000 years after the Fair's first year.

At Westinghouse's World's Fair site on Long Island, they found a narrow well 50 ft. deep, lined it with double steel tubing, stoppered it at the bottom with concrete and sand. The capsule, a cartridge seven and a half feet long, was made of a Westinghouse nickel and silver alloy copper, lined with Pyrex glass, emptied of air, filled with inert nitrogen. Among the objects which went into it were a woman's hat, razor, can opener, fountain pen, pencil, tobacco pouch with zipper, pipe, tobacco, cigarettes, camera, eyeglasses, toothbrush; cosmetics, textiles, metals and alloys; coal, building materials, synthetic plastics, seeds; dictionaries, language tests, magazines (*Time* among them), other written records on microfilm. In order to make reasonably sure that archaeologists of 6939 would know of the treasure consigned to them, Westinghouse sent books of record to the world's leading libraries, telling how to calculate the date when the capsule should be opened, by use of the Gregorian, Chinese, Jewish, Mohammedan and Shint calendars, and by astronomical time if no calendars survive. Also given were the exact latitude and longitude of the capsule's well, calculated to less than an inch. In case the latitude and longitude figures should be falsified by continental creep, directions were given for locating the capsule with electro-magnetic finders.

For two years Fairgoers have gaped at the capsule, gleaming at the bottom of its open well. One day this week, from a huge, hot cauldron, 500 lb. of petroleum pitch, chlorinated diphenyl and mineral oil were poured into the well, to act as a packing indefinitely resistant to moisture and soil acids. On the stroke of noon, the well was sealed. A crowd of spectators bared their heads. A bugle sounded taps. The capsule started on its long journey through time.

*   *   *

Our civilisation has certainly reached a high level and, today, Earthman has made further big technological strides. He is using nuclear power. Moreover, he has landed several times on the Moon and is preparing to go to other worlds in this solar system.

Nevertheless, scattered all around this planet are landmarks of stone and earth, which have stood for thousands of years, silent sentinels of the vestiges of a far greater civilisation. Classerness in the Isle of Lewis, together with Avebury and the Glastonbury area in Britain; Carnac in Brittany; Easter Island in the Pacific; Tiahuanaco, near Lake Titicaca, in the high Andes of South America; the cyclopean monuments of the Deccan in India; the hills and barrows made by the Mound Builders of America. All these places and many more bear witness to a mighty civilisation of such proportions that our own much vaunted one pales into insignificance beside it.

In nearly all these areas are traces of both solar and serpent worship. The two went together. The sun being considered the outward manifestation of the Godhead and the serpent as the Word which called all life into existence. The evidence shows that all these remains of past cultures stem from one source – from one parent civilisation.

The Ancient Egyptians, whose rulers considered themselves descended from the Sun-God, built great pyramids. They had wonderful jewellery and ceramics. They were especially fond of gold. They practised mummification. They installed along the banks of the Nile a wonderful irrigation system for agriculture.

Across the Atlantic Ocean in South America, the Incas of Ancient Peru also claimed descent from the Sun-Gods and were regarded like the Pharaohs of Egypt as Divine Rulers. The word Inca means Emperor. The Incas ruled over many tribes, including the Quichua. This great civilisation constructed enormous cyclopean buildings at Huarez, Tiahuanaco and Cuzco. According to the late Sir Banister Fletcher, their masonry was superb and similar to early Etruscan work.[4] This is a very interesting comparison. How is it that Inca architecture should have such close similarity to that of a mysterious race in Central Italy known as the Etruscans?

The Inca civilisation created wonderful pottery and beautiful jewellery. Around Lake Titicaca were to be found many valuable minerals, including gold. The Incas installed enormous irrigation systems for agriculture, with rows of terraces climbing up the sides of the Andes. They, also, like the Ancient Egyptians on the other side of the Atlantic, practised mummification.

The Mayan and Toltec civilisations which flourished in Mexico and Central America also worshipped the sun. These people too built huge pyramids, many-storeyed temples called 'Teocallis'. Fletcher compared them to the Ziggurats of Babylon.[5] Once again, striking similarities of unusual architecture built by ancient peoples on both sides of the Atlantic. The Maya had no wheels, only sledges. They also had no iron, so their tools were either of wood or stone. All the more fantastic that they erected such huge buildings! Could the Maya, the Ancient Egyptians, the Babylonians and other races of long ago, have used some form of levitation, to enable them to move great pieces of masonry into place, similar to what is being achieved on a smaller scale by the science of sonics today?

In India, huge megaliths were built by a race in ancient times that also mined gold. They also found other metals, including iron. They settled in these mining areas and installed irrigation systems for their agriculture.

Let us look farther. In Japan, the Land of the Rising Sun, are to be found, according to W. J. Perry, ancient irrigation systems near gold mining areas, along with pyramids and dolmens around the Upper Yeneisi.[6] Japan's Mikados or Emperors, also, claim descent from the Sun.

All over the world are to be found the same things – the same pattern – this extraordinary sun-worshipping civilisation with its pyramids, dolmens and stone circles; its mining activities and fondness for gold; its elaborate irrigation systems for food production.

It is a remarkable fact that all the ancient peoples of North, South and Central America, state that they are descended from people who came from the East. Whereas, all
The evidence only too clearly indicates that people went
descended from immigrants who came from the West.
The evidence only too clearly indicates that people went
forth from a central focal point in all directions across the world, seeking new places where there were minerals, to settle and establish their own civilisation. What and where was that central point – that parent source of civilisation?

Most authorities consider that the Mediterranean was the cradle of culture and acknowledge Ancient Egypt as the parent. Is such a widely held view necessarily correct? There is evidence which should be taken into account, pointing to the Atlantic Ocean and the British Isles, as the home base from which the Phoenicians, the Celts and others, went forth to show the world how to sail ships, to produce food, to make beer, to mine minerals, to erect pyramids and other cyclopean buildings. These, I submit, were the Atlanteans who colonised the world. Furthermore, the British people, as we shall see, together with their American descendants, are of Atlantean extraction.

Atlantis – that magnificent Empire of the Sun – went down beneath the waters of the Atlantic Ocean, probably in three main stages. There is reason to consider that a tremendous seismic upheaval occurred on the Earth's surface at approximately 25000 BC, there is strong evidence that there was another around 13000 BC, and finally, the Island of Poseid (we have the account of Plato) was submerged about 9500 BC. However, the British Isles remain!

Occult tradition infers that the Atlanteans had probably reached a very high degree of technological achievement prior to 25000 BC. Undoubtedly they had space ships and were in communication with other planets. Their civilisation which originally had been on sound lines gradually grew more materialistic. Atlantean scientists were playing with forces capable of the most terrible destructive potential – even more so than the nuclear ones with which madmen frighten the world in our own times. They started a full-scale war and unleashed a chain-reaction of lethal power far beyond their ability to keep under control. This holocaust resulted in seismic disturbances that ended in the destruction of the greater part of Atlantis. Huge tidal waves swept across the world – land masses shifted – and large portions of the population perished.

Since then there have been two other major catastrophes affecting Atlantis. H. S. Bellamy advanced the theories of Hans Hoerbiger as to how another planet in this solar system, Luna, was captured by the earth and became its present satellite, our Moon. This cosmic event began about 15,000 years ago and, according to Bellamy and Hoerbiger, caused the sudden draining of the Mongolian Sea.[7] This tremendous flood of water poured into the Black Sea and broke through the Bosporus to create the Mediterranean Sea which was not previously there. These events, coupled with climatic changes, altered the face of the globe. The continuous wrenching, twisting and turning of the Earth in this gargantuan cosmic upheaval with Luna, caused faults to form on the face of the world and mountains to arise on its surface. The Rocky Mountains, the Cascade Range and the Andes, in the Americas, together with the Himalayas in Asia and the Alps in Europe, were either not there previously or had not achieved anything like their present range and height. Immanuel Velikovsky wrote that 'The great massif of the Himalayas rose to its present height in the age of modern, actually historical, man.'[8]

The remains of a deserted city lie 12,000 feet up in the Andes. This is Tiahuanaco, with its great monolithic structures made of 200-ton stones. It lies at the same height and not far from Lake Titicaca. When the catastrophe came, with the

21

sudden rising of the Andes, following the inrush of tidal waves over the land, Tiahuanaco was carried bodily up from its position by the sea to its present high elevation!

A Russian scientist, Alexandre Kazantsev, recently wrote that the lake, too, was lifted to its present altitude by a natural cataclysm and was formerly an inlet of the sea. If you visit Lake Titicaca today the old shore line can still be seen where, says Kazantsev, shells and other marine plants may be found, which confirm that the lake was originally part of the sea.

Furthermore, Kazantsev claims the remains of a seaport may still be distinguished. He points out that not far from Tiahuanaco are the cyclopean ruins constructed of gigantic blocks of stone, and makes the apt comment that to transport such masonry up to such an altitude even in our modern day and age would be an impossible and unimaginable task.

Outstanding among these gigantic ruins is the Gateway of the Sun, on which is carved a figure of the Sun, surrounded by winged messengers. More than any other example, the Gates of the Sun present us with far from simple stones. The lintel of these gates is carved in fantastical aesthetic, highly thought out, mathematical, and, if we are to credit the findings of capable astronomers in our own time, almost unbelievably accurate so-called decorations.

On the gateway is sculptured a very strange, but extremely precise astronomical calendar. Kazantsev estimates the Sun Gate to have been built between 12,000-15,000 years ago. For 15,000 years, he says, our earth has turned on its axis at *practically* the same speed. But why, he asks, should this calendar be so different from our own known ones?

The Tiahuanaco calendar shows a year of 290 days (not 365), composed of twelve months (ten of twenty-four days, that is 240; and two of twenty-five days, that is 50). The Russian scientist states that Professor Girov and others have agreed that the Tiahuanaco calendar is the oldest in the world. Kazantsev relates a most thought-provoking incident. Two Soviet newspapers, *Pravda* and *Izvestia*, both printed an article from the Academy of Sciences of the USSR, signed by V. Kotelvihov and Professor I. Chklovski. According to these scientists, Venus has been found to rotate on her axis in eleven earth days, if the planet's axis is not inclined to the plane of her orbit. If one accepts the findings of the American investigator, Cooper, on the inclination of Venus's axis, writes Kazantsev, the period of her rotation would be a little more than nine earth days. So, that in a Venusian year there would be 225 earth days. In short, the Venusian year would comprise twenty-four Venusian days! Kazantsev points to the Tiahuanaco calendar in which each month has twenty-four earth days. Was it right, he asks, to look upon the Tiahuanaco little cycle as months?

'It could be it was not a month at all, but a *year*! Is it difficult to conjecture the whole number of days in a year? The terrestrial year is not composed of an entire number of days, 365¼. Every four years one adds a year of 366 days. The terrestrial year balances itself there. And the Venusian? For the moment, we know that the period of rotation of Venus is nine earth days. But if 290 days go exactly into a twelve-year cycle? There would thus be ten Venusian years of twenty-four days each and two years (bi-sextiles) of twenty-five days. And this corresponds exactly to the Tiahuanaco calendar. If this is a coincidence it is an astounding one.'[9]

So, the amazing possibility confronts us, was the Tiahuanaco calendar Venusian? If so, the significance of this is very important.

We know that some tremendous catastrophe occurred causing a whole city and a lake to be transported 12,000 feet up in the mountains, and for the construction of the monoliths to remain unfinished. H. H. Wilkins quoted an ancient legend of the Aymara Indians of Bolivia and Peru.

'After a long night there dawned,
standing upright to the eyes of our
forefathers, the great ruins you now see.'[10]

Tiahuanaco stands today, a silent deserted monument to the mysterious people who built it. What happened to them? Did they all perish, or were they able to escape in time?

Scores of the South Sea Islands in the Pacific Ocean contain the remains of enormous stone temples, megaliths, stone-lined canals and roads, constructed long ago by an unknown race. Could it be that the builders of Tiahuanaco were able to reach Papeete or Easter Island, both of which are in the South Seas and on which similar giant statuary was erected? The huge stone structures on Easter Island were also left unfinished and in such a manner as to indicate they had to be suddenly abandoned.

The well-known writer and explorer, Thor Heyerdahl, made his famous *Kon-Tiki* expedition on a raft from South America to the South Seas. Mr Heyerdahl considers that the people who erected the 550 colossal stone figures of men, gazing disdainfully inland, on the tall cliffs of Easter Island, were the same race of people who built mysterious Tiahuanaco. He further concludes that they probably journeyed to the South Seas in much the same way as he did.[11]

On the other hand, the builders of Tiahuanaco, and the people who constructed the giant figures on Easter Island, may both have been colonists from Atlantis, and quite conceivably in communication. The Great Catastrophe that occurred about 13000 BC was one that encompassed most of the world, and the inhabitants of both places may well have perished suddenly at approximately the same time.

It is known that these fantastic figures on Easter Island are all, with one exception, of men. One stone statue of a woman was found lying face downwards in the centre of the island. The faces of the men are not the same. They are all of different individuals, but all have the same large eyes and big foreheads. Almost every figure has very long ears. This is especially interesting as the Orejones – fighting men of the ancient Incas – were also long-eared.

Wilkins relates how strange catacombs hidden in the cliffs of Easter Island were found to contain human remains and on the walls were frescoes of a 'queer animal of prehistoric sort, which has a cat's head and the curved form of a man with a bent back and long thin arms'. He wrote that 'Zoology and geology know of no such prehistoric monster; but it was also found on pieces of very ancient pottery dug up on the shores of South Peru.' Certainly, there is some very close connection between Tiahuanaco and Easter Island!

To complete the trio of unfinished massive cyclopean buildings in widely separated parts of the world are the ruins of Baalbeck, which lie at a height of 3,500 feet, to the north-east of Beirut. The Romans built magnificent temples to their gods upon, in the words of Mark Twain, 'massive sub-structures that might support a world almost. The material used is blocks of stone as large as an omnibus. . . .'

The main ruins consist of the Great Temple, as well as the Temples of Venus, Bacchus and Jupiter. The Great Temple, which according to Fletcher was constructed by the Romans, AD 131-161, in the reign of Antonius Pius 'forms part of the magnificent temple group which rears its massive form high above the plain, below the hills of Lebanon, and stands as a testimony to the power of Roman rule in Syria and to the establishment of Roman State religion wherever the legionaries planted the Imperial standards. It was raised on a high platform, approached by steps which led to a dodecastyle Corinthian portica "in antis".'[12]

The massive sub-structures, referred to by Mark Twain, and which form the huge platform on which the Great Temple is built, are truly amazing. He wrote that one stretch of the platform, composed of only three stones, was nearly 200 feet in length! They are thirteen feet square, two of them being sixty-four feet and the third sixty-nine feet long, and built into the massive wall twenty feet above the ground.

No one, so far, has come up with the answer as to who built the massive platform at Baalbeck, upon which the Romans are known to have constructed a very long time afterwards their wonderful temples.

In their own time the Romans were in exactly the same position as modern authority. Jupiter, Saturn, Juno and all the rest of the Pantheon were, to the Romans, representations of the Ultimate, or functions of the Ultimate in the knowable Universe. The fact that the Romans were able, in one way or another, to enforce this opinion, paved the way to what we now call our modern civilisation. It laid the groundwork for the scientific age.

The Romans managed to stamp out the last remains of their Atlantean heritage of culture, and because they were able to set themselves up as the originators of civilisation, they have been called the civilisers of every succeeding era since their time.

Of course, the Greeks have been called in, but that is only

because the Romans got the life of their own culture from them. The Greeks, then, could not be entirely obliterated. They were essentially philosophers, and were only soldiers when they had to be, under the circumstances current in their world. And, in this reference, it can be pointed out that no Athenian would have liked to admit that any Spartan was really a proper, acceptable Greek. That idea came along later, with the advent of the British public school.

It happens to be a matter of interpretation. Each succeeding age interprets the preceding one to its own best advantage and, particularly, if it be an age of Warriors, is motivated primarily by the simple, fundamental (if animal) goal: to survive.

Essentially, this is an egotistical goal, and therefore, really no goal at all, but a false one. Out of striving for this goal we derive the ideas of service and of sacrifice. Neither are natural to Man, as we consider him, that is, as an Inhabitant of the Universe, created by the Great Architect Himself – not to be a slave, a sycophant, a companion or an equal – but simply because the Great Universal Intelligence decided, one bright and sunny Eternity when he felt that way, to Make Something.

Why must we be like God? (If, indeed, we must.) Why aren't we good enough to be what we are? Must chemical man always try to usurp his elder brother's birthright? And must humanity always try to behave like Lucifer and take over the administration of Heaven?

Is it because we have literally nowhere to go in that direction to seek a goal? Have we made goal-seeking our goal? What will happen to us if we have done that? When a rubber ball hits a concrete wall, it bounces back. When goal-seeking can no longer expand, it must invert its direction and contract. If one can no longer look *out*, then one must, perforce, look *within*, or give up looking.

When the natural limits of building upward and outward are reached, then each attempted addition to the construction becomes a means of destruction. The house of cards is finally toppled by the impossible attempt to add just one more card. The camel's back cracks under the impact of the last and insupportable straw.

The fact, cold, hard and material, is that in various places around the world there are remains of cyclopean masonry of a size and form that could not be contemplated today, with all our mechanical aids and developments.

The stones of Baalbeck: the Gate of the Sun at Tiahuanaco: the impossible stones of Cuzco. To say nothing of the Pyramids. The gist of observation reveals that at some time in the history of our planet, such building was taken as a matter of course. The Gate of the Sun at Tiahuanaco stands in silent testimony of this fact. Not only did the builders consider their architecture as a possibility to be achieved – they took the building of this gate for granted. It was their natural approach to an architectural problem. It was their common, ordinary, everyday, garden variety of procedure. How do we know this, and how can we be so definite about it?

Let us apply the rule of the simplest solution – this time to a mental and emotional problem (since we have no idea whatever about the means they used to achieve the physical, chemical world motions necessary to the erection of this wonder we are considering).

The people, whoever they may have been, that set up the Gate of the Sun were building according to the way 'people built' in their day and time. We could compare them to any member in good standing of the Bricklayers' Union in any great city of the world in our own time, who might be called upon to erect a brick wall. He would know what was to be done with the material at hand, how to do it and would take the job. And it would be done well.

Astronomical dating leaves us to suppose that this was what happened at Tiahuanaco. How can we be sure?

Let us look again at the Gate of the Sun. They are not just simple stones. It is equally impossible to say of some of the other megaliths that puzzle us nowadays that they are simple stones, when we pause to consider the means by which they were made and erected.

The quarry from which these colossal stones at Baalbeck were taken is a quarter of a mile away from the platform and at a much lower level. Mark Twain relates how in a pit lay a similar stone, 'the mate of the largest stone in the ruins'.

27

What is more, it lies there 'squared and ready for the builder's hands, a solid mass fourteen feet by seventeen feet wide and seventy feet long'.

What caused that tremendous block of masonry intended for the great solid platform at Baalbeck to be abandoned, leaving the work unfinished?

And it lies there where they left it when suddenly 'called away from their labour'. Since they were such honest workmen, let us hope they were called away to their refreshment. We cannot be sure, but impressed by the sheer grandeur of their work, it is to be sincerely hoped that this is what occurred.

At any rate, their stone lies where it does because the Romans, who built upon the unfinished platform where the original builders had taken its sister stones, had no means of moving it all that way up a hill to make any practical use of it. Certainly, had they been able to shift it, they would have taken the stone on up to the platform, and worked it into the underpinnings along with the others they had found already there.

Baalbeck may well be the key and the clue to what has been going on in this world. If it is, Baalbeck may, in time, reveal the multiple lock which has kept mankind from knowing what Man has been trying to show him for a very, very long time.

In and for their own age, the Romans were as civilised as we are. Would-be teachers and preachers in our own times try to tell us that materialism and commercialism are ruining the world. They impress on us that we are living in a modern Babylon. Well enough. Perhaps we are. But, it is a modern Babylon, and not the same one the prophets fulminated against.

This means that the outward forms and usages are different, now. It is the same old Christmas Tree, but with an entirely new set of decorations. The basic conditions, the essential framework, make such a similar picture that no mind trained to the first degree of logic would dare refute, let alone reject that correspondence.

Modernism is a matter of form. It is a matter of How Things Look, and The Way Things Are Done. Modernism is always, in any day and for any age, a matter of the time. The best of the so-called modern painters in Chelsea or anywhere else are using pigments in a way that would have turned the Old Masters quite green with envy. No Old Master ever had such colour or such potential permanence at hand with such ease of achievement.

So it is with all of us, in each of the different departments of our daily lives. And, so it is with the scientific people who are avidly exploring the chemical universe, for once in complete freedom, and without their being told by any other authority that they cannot see or that they cannot *make* something.

We do not know, and therefore cannot say, for certain, whether the work referred to here was being done at the cataclysmic part of the Grand Cycle, that is, around 13000 BC, or if some of it was still continuing when Poseid went down about 9500 BC.

In the case of the earlier cataclysm, it is possible that the architects of Tiahuanaco, or at least some people who had been in touch with them were still there. At the latter date, 9500 BC, it is likely that tradition alone was the motivating force, coupled, of course, with what remained of the old Atlantean technology.

Whatever the facts may have been, when the later constructions were made, the builders, at least, had remembered. They had maintained the tradition of the Artisan that is handed down from father to son and from son to grandson. They still knew how to look at the earth, to find the place where the essential stone lay concealed and unnoticed, passed over, beneath the soil. They knew how to clear away the débris, and how to come down to the basic building material. They were also very sure of themselves within the discipline of their own particular craft. They knew how to cut that basic material and make it useful to the architecture they were contemplating.

They could find what they wanted, and, quite without benefit of the internal combustion engine or any other product of the modern machine-shop, cheerfully chop out stone blocks nearly seventy feet long, tow them a quarter of a mile uphill, and set them in a row. Yes, a row the Romans thought worthy to build upon in their own way, and upon which to erect temples for the greatest and most respected of their gods.

The Romans never cut out and never transported the original (and to the Romans) sacred stones. The obvious proof of this lies a quarter of a mile downhill from the spot upon which those Romans erected their magnificent and unequalled temples.

The proof is a silent and immovable stone.

2. Giants from the Sky

But what's the idea behind it all? – *Conway*

Tiahuanaco, Easter Island and other examples of cyclopean constructions, remain unexplained enigmas for fascinating conjecture. However, I suggest they may all have been abandoned at the same time and for the same reason. A sudden, overwhelming, terrifying catastrophe such as occurred in 13000 BC, and which caused people to flee for their very lives.

There is a tradition that about 13000 BC the planetary orbit of Earth was more elliptical than it is now. One part of it was close to the orbit of Luna, then the third true planet from the Sun. The various orbital speeds of the planets involved sometimes brought the Earth very close to Luna. Sometimes, Luna appeared in earthly skies as a bright lunar body – at other times she was absent. Mythology refers to her as Diana, the Huntress, and she was accompanied by her own two moons – her 'hounds'. Venus came closer at times, too, and appeared as a *very* bright star.

This strange distortion of Earth's orbit persisted long enough for stories of it to live on in Greek and Red Indian legends, and to produce great reverence for and emphasis upon Venus as the Morning and Evening Star.

Furthermore, when close conjunction between Earth and Luna occurred they produced eruptions – great and devastating tidal effects, and disruptions on the surface of the world.

Earth captured one of Luna's moons. It split in two and crashed into the Earth. This happened around 13000 BC. The other moon exploded in the distorted magnetic field and its fragments destroyed the surface of Luna, nearly stopping her rotation.

It is significant that W. Peck, writing in his erudite astronomical book, plumped for the naming and mapping of the signs of the zodiac in the heavens, as dating from about

31

15,000 years ago, that is, 13000 BC.[13] Is it not strange, too, that Kazantsev estimated The Gateway of the Sun at Tiahuanaco, with its 'out of this world' calendar should have been constructed between 12,000-15,000 years ago? Peck's date corresponds surprisingly well with the supposed date of the Earth's finally settling down into a stable orbit around the Sun somewhere in between those of Venus and Luna, with the probable epoch (possibly long sustained and drawn out) of the final capture of Luna, which was not complete until 9500 BC, and was the cause of the sinking of Poseid.

After the convulsions and upheavals the Earth had just been through, it is more than likely that the stars and planets would not appear from here to be in the same positions in the sky, and such a settling down of the heavens – for so the event must have seemed from the point of view of Earth – would provide an occasion, at long last, to establish a new, meaningful and useful map of the sky.

It is interesting to note that at about 13000 BC, there was no star as near the pole as Polaris is now. Vega, the bright star in the constellation of Lyra, would appear to describe a small circle in the Northern Sky. It will be doing the same in about 11,500 years hence.

At the next Earth-Luna conjunction, Earth captured Luna as her own moon. This happened around 9500 BC, and was the cause of another major catastrophe on the Earth's surface, accompanied by more tidal waves and movements of land masses, including the submergence of Poseid, the famous Atlantean island. The sinking of Poseid is described by Plato in his Dialogues.

All this has given the Moon a very bad reputation and a definite connection with evil. In many parts of the world people still believe that to sleep in the rays of the full moon drives men mad. Could not this be a folk-memory from the time when the Moon was responsible for so much tragedy in the world?

Many people find it difficult to believe that the Moon has not always been our satellite. Nevertheless, there are many legends and lingering memories among many races of the time when not the Moon but Venus shone brightly on us. Wilkins wrote: 'It is curious that the Ancient Mexicans spoke of the planet Venus as lighting the Eastern Skies and not the Moon.' He also records the Indians of the high savannas of Colombia as saying, 'The Great Catastrophe befell the Earth before the Moon shone in the skies.'

The weight of this new system of 'sister planets' readjusted Earth's orbit to the Solar System's magnetic field to something like its present position. She slowed down – is still slowing down. As this readjustment continued, Earth's year increased from about 290 days, first to 360 and then to the present 365¼. The length of a whole year in present time compared with what it was in ancient times, may well explain the ripe old ages that Methuselah and other biblical patriarchs reached.

When you consider this whole situation, our present Moon is *relatively* much too big – compared with the moons of other planets – to be a genuine satellite!

Some time passed before the captured planet, Luna, settled down in her new orbit as our Moon, and for centuries tidal waves and eruptions on the earth's surface harassed the bemused survivors. The population of the world after this series of catastrophes was very small. Those that were left had been driven almost insane and reduced to a state where they were little more than terrified animals. They never knew when another violent paroxysm of the earth might occur, causing hot lava to erupt out of cavities, tidal waves to overwhelm them or earthquakes to swallow them up.

Most of the survivors, because of the state of their minds, and the hopelessness for some time after the catastrophe of trying to establish themselves in any particular place, wandered about the earth seeking their food wherever it could be found. People were unable to keep any system of agriculture going due to the centuries of unpredictable weather conditions, and finally, the art of agriculture was completely lost. They were reduced to a wandering, hunting and fishing state.

One part of Atlantis had not gone under. The lands now known as the British Isles – the Fortunate Isles – remained high and dry, and it was from there that the world was once more to receive civilisation.

The Atlanteans had foreseen the destruction of Poseid and built, in conjunction with the Sky People, a gigantic landmark, which could easily be picked out from the sky on the disrupted surface of the unhappy planet. Where did they construct such a place with a reasonable chance of survival?

Atlantis may have been an Empire, world-wide, and some of us believe it was. But Poseid was an island. When people say 'Atlantis' they usually mean Poseid. Thus, when speaking of the submergence of Atlantis, they generally mean the final disappearance of the last remnant of the old Mother Country in the Atlantic, that is, Poseid, which is said to have sunk about 9564 BC.

The final sinking could not have been totally unexpected, although the people of that time probably didn't have a timetable on the event and so did not know exactly when to expect it.

Most of what has been written and remembered about the occurrence (that is, most of what I have had access to) tells us it happened fairly quickly once the big upheaval started. By the third day it was almost over. After that, about all that was left were the Azores, and they must have been almost uninhabitable for some time.

Left in the memory of the evacuees was the image of an island (one main one and a few small, surrounding ones) that had suddenly become *The Land of the Dead*, or, *The Isles of the Dead*.

And so this area has been handed down in history and tradition into our own time. Somewhere to the west lay the Isles of the Dead, the land where all were dead – the lost, drowned land to which the Sun apparently sank at the end of the day, when it disappeared into the Western Ocean.

From this concept it is only one short mental jump to the idea that The Land of the Dead being the land where all are dead, then it must be that it is the very land to which departed souls of people who die must go. Reality, suitably diluted by time, with an added dash of ecclesiastical explanation would seem to make this clear.

Northward, there was another piece of country which had been part of the old Atlantean Empire. It was partly connected to the European mainland and partly not. There were many small islands in the group – one large one, Ireland – and a peninsula thrusting out from the European mainland, shaped something like a boot. This area may have rocked a bit, changed some of its contours, but it did not sink, like poor old Poseid.

Therefore, in the thinking of the survivors, the inhabitants of this northerly set of islands and other country, were especially favoured. They must have been specially blessed by the gods and preserved in the face of catastrophe.

And, because people thought about this area in that way, they began to call these northwesterly islands, *The Fortunate Islands*, or *The Isles of the Blest*. And that name stuck too.

Then, as time went by, apparently the two locations became confused in the minds of people who had never been there. The names of the two areas, Poseid and the British Isles with its peninsula (which later on did become an island at the appearance of the English Channel), collapsed together and became the name of one 'mythical' place. People thought about the Isles of the Dead and the Fortunate Isles or Isles of the Blest, as being one and the same. They came to be considered very probably legendary and belonging to the next world, and therefore (very probably), invisible to mortal eyes.

This is the historical confusion we must learn to untangle. However, the point here is not history, but the sacred character of islands. As the drowned and lost Motherland, Poseid became a sacred island. The British group was already sacred, even in Atlantean times, as 'The Imperishable Island' (they were saying, even back then, in their own way and for their own reasons: There'll always be an England) – or, as 'The Dry Island,' the reliable piece of territory that always managed to keep its head above water, no matter what happened to the rest of the world.

This set of islands was venerated not only as an ancient home of Man on Earth, but also on account of its geographical location. Most of all, it was looked upon as sacred because it was the site of The Great Temple of the Stars – the 'earthly' zodiac in Somerset.

Between what are now Glastonbury and Somerton, our Atlantean ancestors carved giant effigies out of the soil. These are also delineated by water courses and ancient pathways, and form a circular replica of the zodiacal sky above. How many people in Britain, let alone the world, know of this great, incomparable, Kingdom of Knowledge, Wisdom and Truth, that is contained in this 'earthly Garden of Eden'?

When the true significance and understanding of the Somerset Zodiac is really grasped, the British people will realise that they have on their soil a monument from the past, which will help them to understand not only the present but also the future. *A legacy from their Atlantean forebears which is infinitely greater than either Stonehenge or the Great Pyramid in Egypt.*

The research done by Mrs Maltwood on these prehistoric earthworks is, therefore, of inestimable value, and that is why a fair amount of space is devoted to it here. I would add that when I visited the Somerset Zodiac recently, further data was found, which will not only help to confirm Mrs Maltwood's work but also add to the significance of the whole conception.

Most people are to some extent familiar with the story of King Arthur and his Round Table. Mrs Maltwood, in her book, quotes extensively from a translation of the *High History of the Holy Graal.*[14] She brings out the important point that King Arthur and his Round Table represent the Circle of the Zodiac. She also refers to another French work which has this to say about the Round Table:

'The Round Table was constructed, not without great significance, upon the advice of Merlin. By its name the Round Table is meant to signify the round world and round canopy of the planets and the elements, in the firmament, where are to be seen the stars and many other things.'[15]

Mrs Maltwood describes not only each zodiacal giant lying on the ground, but relates how the *High History of the Holy Graal* refers to it. We are dealing here not with the Christian Grail, for the zodiacal giants were constructed, as will be seen, many thousands of years before the Coming of Jesus, the Christ. *One reason why Joseph of Arimathea later came to Glastonbury with the Christian relics was because it was already the most sacred spot on Earth.*

The pre-Christian Grail 'mystery', according to Mrs Maltwood, appeared to have been 'three knights and King Arthur representing the sun in the four quarters of the year, within the "Golden Round" each having his own "house" or constellation giant, . . .'16

Mrs Maltwood's advice to prove the correspondence of the Earth Giants with the celestial constellations as they are depicted by astronomers today, is to lay Philip's Planisphere – which is the same size – on the back of the effigy chart of the heavens– and to prick the stars through. If the square of Ursa Minor be laid on the 'giant dragon's' head, at the centre of the circle; with Aldebaran on the equinoctial to the west, and Antares on the same line to the east; then the rest of the stars will fall as indicated on the Earth Chart.

Referring to the Earth Chart, Mrs Maltwood states: 'Is it remarkable that the stars which agree with their corresponding constellation figures on the ground, only lie along the celestial path of the sun, moon and planets: with the notable exception of the Giants Hercules and Orion, whose stars also fit their correct effigies, when transferred from the modern Planisphere on to the map of Somerset.'17

There is no way to determine from this cryptic note if Mrs Maltwood had any ideas about just what this strange but pointed pair of exceptions could mean if its symbology is applied to the two divisions of the human race. Full and frank discussions of 'The Twins' and the derivations of the twin symbol that plays such a prominent part in the history of humanity are few and far between. In this book we will be going into this important aspect later on. But here we have the two 'giants' again, in the form of the heavenly member of the duo, Orion, and the earthly member, Hercules, and in the effigy system their stars, when pricked through the Planisphere fall within the figures on the ground. Indeed, Orion, the Heavenly Twin, holds one of the two chief stars of the zodiacal constellation Gemini (The Twins) 'on his uplifted right hand', while Hercules, who represents the Earthly Twin, has fallen face downward into the Zodiac because the 'horse' he is riding has stumbled under him!

It should be pointed out that of the genuine zodiacal constellations, not all are represented in the Somerset Temple of Stars in exactly the same figures with which we are familiar today. We know that the Zodiac we now possess, with its twelve signs all equally divided around the Circle, comes to us from Egypt and the Eastern Mediterranean. From that area, apparently, it went eastward in the form given it there, and became the twelve-signed Zodiacs of India and China. This seems to have happened first among the priests, and it was not until the power of the priesthood began to wane that twelve signs were openly discussed among laymen and exoteric astrologers. Earlier only *ten* were talked about, two being withheld as sacred and secret, although, of course, all twelve were well known to the initiated.

We have seen, above, that Orion takes the place of part of the modern representation of Gemini, the Twins. In the map of the sky only the Heavenly Twin appears in effigy at the place of the twins in the sky. What could say more plainly, that *one of the twins is in the sky*. The other, remember, is being thrown face downward to the Earth by his inadequate and stumbling horse, which, by the way, is being stung by the Scorpion!

The other twin, Hercules, is associated then, with the constellation Saggitarius, who is actually represented by the Centaur drawing a bow. When the Scythians came down out of the north on horseback, the early Greeks were terrified of them, mistaking horse and rider for a single animal, and inventing by mistake this half-man, half-horse monster. In the Temple of the Stars it is Hercules, the Earth-born semi-divine hero who rides the stumbling horse. 'All the greater stars of Saggitarius fall in the hind-quarters of the horse.'

Thus, we can trace our modern symbol for Sagittarius back to the early Greek people, who first invented the Centaur and then adopted the horse themselves. After they adopted the horse, of course, the Centaur became a mythical figure with certain supernatural associations derived from history.

The Somerset Zodiac, by showing a horse and a rider at the position of Sagittarius shows at once a relationship with the Zodiacs the Greeks knew, one which they either borrowed from the Egyptians or derived with the Egyptians from a common source. Which, then, came first? The Mediterranean Zodiac with its twelve signs, or the Somerset Zodiac with its *ten* effigies corresponding to the Circle of the Zodiac.

The answer must surely be an immediate and unequivocal: The Somerset Zodiac came first, and very possibly by many millennia. By the time the Greeks got their Zodiac, the esoteric character of the whole idea had been lost. Any representation of the zodiac that contains all twelve constellations represented as separate signs and given separate symbolic figures is an exoteric Zodiac. It is the product of a time when the earlier statements of knowledge had succumbed to 'modern' disclosure, popularisation and revision.

The earlier Zodiacs would have shown only *ten* figures, and this is the case at The Temple of the Stars in Somerset. There are ten effigies in the Circle of the Sun. When this great temple was erected for all to see it was still customary to represent the zodiacal constellations by only ten figures publicly . . . and this is exactly what we find.

Thus, the Somerset circle is older, probably by far, than any Mediterranean Zodiac, be it Egyptian, Greek or Babylonian. The Mediterranean people were the disseminators of wisdom and knowledge, the publicisers and the revisers. Knowing that there were twelve constellations, but having forgotten why there were two that were 'veiled', they reconstructed the symbols to bring out all twelve. Profane knowledge appeared to move a step ahead, progress was made – and the real 'whys and wherefores' became even more esoteric or covered up than they had been before. When people think they know everything they do not bother to enquire into the past.

In the geography of the Somerset Zodiac, the tongue of the dragon is shown casting up the ship, the constellation Argo. In this ship sits the giant, Orion.

Mrs Maltwood says of this giant: 'Orion takes the place of one of the Twins in Somerset: two of the stars of that constellation fall on his right hand, and he is the house of the Sun which was Twin to the Moon. In Egypt he figured both as Osiris and Horus, while in Persian representations of Gemini, Orion himself, or his giant head, is shown between the Twins.'[18]

Orion, then, represents the Heavenly Twin.

Where, then, is his brother in human shape? The other stars of Gemini fall not on a human effigy but upon the mask of Leo, the Lion, long a symbol of the Earthly Brother.

The effigy of the other Twin Giant, the Earthly Brother is displaced. He is Hercules, the demi-god, who is half human and half god. We find him, as already stated, in the Somerset Zodiac, riding upon the stumbling horse of Sagittarius, falling headlong into the earthly counterpart of the sky. He is Hercules . . . and Hercules is The Arthur, father of the line or chain of Arthurs which culminated in that last of the hierarchy whom John Whitehead calls 'Guardian of the Grail'.[19]

Hours of fruitful meditation could be based upon the symbology apparent in this arrangement of the figures. It is full of meaning and tells a large part of the great story of mankind. From the characteristics of the figures as they lie before us in the Somerset Zodiac, it is apparent that there is something unnatural and abnormal about these Twins. In our own exoteric zodiac, as astrology has it now, the Twins are shown as two human figures, often as children, twin boys. The true, esoteric concept lies hidden behind this contemporary veil, and it is figured for us by the giant effigies.

In the Somerset Zodiac, the constellation we now call The Twins is divided between the figure of Orion and the figure of the Lion. Because the ancient idea has been exotericised, the twin image in our zodiac was developed into the symbol we have today. The concept has survived, but the old interpretation of it is as esoteric today, as it was when the Somerset Zodiac was erected. Esoteric ideas have a way of remaining esoteric, no matter how much apparent publicity they are given. Those who have eyes, see, and those who have ears, hear. The rest of the population brings the symbology down in time, into a period and a history it can comprehend.

Mythology is shorthand. It is condensed history, and it lives on in analogy. The truth behind a myth is always broader and more cosmic in its meaning than the simple story that survives, because it is easy to tell and appears to relate to something more directly and immediately connected with the history of the people who are telling it.

So, what do the figures in the Somerset Zodiac tell us about the Two who came to be called The Twins? First, that they were associated, but different. One was Man. He is the Sky Person who is cast up in the earthly sphere. He arrives in *a ship*. The ship is Argo, and Argo is cognate with Ark.

Two of the stars of Gemini fall on his right hand. The other stars of Gemini fall upon the effigy of the Lion. Nearby, almost between them, we find the Griffon delineated. Now, the Griffon is a fabulous animal. He is a manufactured creature. So, we are told in the old stories of Genesis and elsewhere, is animal-man.[20] This Griffon has the head of a bird and the body of a lion.

The bird, in all symbolic languages, is the pictograph of Creative Mind, or, as it is often called in mystical schools, 'spirit'. It represents the ultimate Self of Man. The Griffon has the head of a bird.

The lion, on the other hand, is the King of Beasts, and represents all that is noblest and best in the animal kingdom.

In the Griffon, then, we have a perfect symbolic representation of a creature that unites within himself both a spiritual nature and an animal nature. In plain language, Animal Man.

Orion, bearing in his right hand two stars of the constellation, is the right-hand twin, and he is shown in human form, and, we think, with a halo to further identify him with the Sun and with the Heavenly side of the picture.

The other Man in the Zodiac is Hercules. He is shown as the other Twin, displaced, not in his proper circumstances, fallen, and in difficulty! In connection with the Griffon symbol it is interesting to note that the head of the fallen Hercules lies near a bird, the dove close to the centre of the zodiacal circle around Barton St David. 'The stars that correspond with the outstretched wing, being the important stars in the handle of the "Great Plough",' says Mrs Maltwood.[21]

What more perfect representation could be devised for the originally Heavenly Race of Man, divided into two parts, one still in possession of its rightful heritage, and the other trapped by ignorance and passion in so-called human flesh, to live and die like the animals?

The mistaken association of the self-consciousness with the animal-human body is shown in the development of our zodiacal symbols. In modern zodiacs the constellation of Saggitarius, is shown as a Centaur, half man and half horse. However, in the Somerset Zodiac, the situation is correctly represented. The figure is a horse and rider, which is a very old and esoteric symbol of the actual relationship between a chemical human being and his body, which he wears like a garment.

If one thinks about the past of the Glastonbury area with the idea in mind that St Joseph of Arimathea and other people, including tin-seeking, beer-making, Phoenicians, sailed up to the *Island* of Avalon, it becomes apparent that this part of the country has had – must have had – its geological ups and downs. If one looks into the record, it will be found that this is exactly what has happened.

Not far from Glastonbury, in at least two directions, lie the remains of lake villages. In the present-day village of Glastonbury itself, there is a small museum where one may go and look for as long as one likes at the relics of these lake villages. Pottery, strikingly modern implements, a canoe, a saw that any contemporary carpenter would be proud to own, to say nothing of the famous Glastonbury Bowl – a piece of bronze workmanship that might well have been fabricated in pious imitation of the great Cauldron of Wisdom itself.

The presence of such villages as these assures us of the fact that, in older times, the level of the land lay lower than it does now. But since these older times were merely older, and not the oldest, it may be inferred that they took part (but not too much part) in the final submergence of the mainland of Atlantis – in the downfall of the Island of Poseid. In sympathy, the 'dry island' receded a little way. One might say that it went its scriptural 'mile' (in this case, no more than a step), but not the recommended 'twain'. Like the bowed head at a funeral it acknowledged the departure of a member of the family, but it did not follow that departed kinsman into the grave. For a little while, the land receded and a part of it went under water, at least at high tide. Later on, after its period of mourning, it rose again and became the peaceful pasture-land it is today.

However, not long ago, in the time of the tin-trader, Uncle Joseph of Arimathea (who was also uncle to an Arthur), it was possible to sail not only to the *Island* of Avalon, but practically on up the sea side of the sea goat Capricorn towards Shepton Mallet.

How do we know this?

Great slabs of country like that comprising the British Isles do not sink unevenly or rise unevenly, except where rifts occur. One such rift produced the Irish Sea. Another produced, but much more slowly and less completely, the English Channel. The West Country has moved up and down with these displacements, and in response to the movements of the Atlantic sea-bed, not too differently to the motion, in very slow time, of a solid plank of wood afloat in the Sargasso Sea. At first one side goes down and the other side goes up. Then the other side goes down (as it did in the time of the Roman Arthur, when he was confronted with the problem of the drowning 'Lowland Hundreds'). Then the whole thing moves bodily upwards, and we find ourselves in present time, with both sides of England high and dry, with an English Channel and an Irish Sea.

Fortunately, the Ordnance Survey maps available in England give contours every fifty feet. For our purpose, then, and to give ourselves a margin of error, we can take the fifty feet above sea-level line, colour the area blue, and see more water, probably, than either Joseph of Arimathea or the Ancient Phoenician tin-seekers had to sail in!

Suppose, then, we take an evening off and do just this. What do we find?

Without much imagination, and even with showing the figure to strangers who have not been enlightened as to its source (after the manner of a psychological ink-blot test), most people see the head of a dragon, bearded and fanged, with open mouth and outstretched tongue, flaring nostril and a baleful eye.

If we are at all near to being right in our surmises, the original sense of the Somerset Zodiac was, in part at least, to keep in the memories of the Men of two planets *a purpose, a promise and a prophecy*. The purpose, to maintain a connection between two parts of a race – that of Man – which had to be separated for a time: The promise that these two separated parts would in time come together again to their mutual benefit: And the prophecy of the date and time of that coming back into communication.

If that time of the re-establishment of contact and communication were scheduled to take place somewhere in or near the time of the Age of Aquarius – and, if the beginnings of the preparations for that hoped for time should have been somewhere near the age of the Bull (Taurus), the builders of the Temple would have left signs which they considered would be indisputable. This they must have done. Otherwise, if this point be rejected, once and for all, one might just as well say that the whole of the Zodiac in Somerset is a fortuitous concourse of hills and ditches.

If, on the other hand, it is an acceptable idea that the purpose, the promise and the prophecy are valid, then the Somerset Zodiac is a rune wherein all who run may read. If, as we are told, the Age of Aquarius is to be the age of the regeneration of Man, it is to Glastonbury and to the Temple of the Stars that we must look for information regarding our immediate future.

In the Somerset Zodiac there are certain figures associated with water. The ship, which lies in Somerton Moor, is outlined by drainage canals. At high-tide, even if the water did not come up to the present day fifty-feet contour mark, the ship would disappear. At low-tide it would lie 'beached' again. It is of some importance to realise, in connection with this idea, that no part of the ship, as delineated by Mrs Maltwood, lies above the fifty-feet contour mark, and the same is true of Cetus, the whale, in South Moor. Most of the two fishes of Pisces would have been apparent at all times, either as small islands or near-islands, one connected at the tail to the Lamb's head at Street, and the other connected by the tail to the Isle of Avalon itself, and very probably forming a peninsula of that island, stretching out toward the south-west.

The Isle of Avalon would have been very definitely a separate island, and disregarding the extension, or peninsula of Wearyall Hill (the northern Fish of Pisces), the main part of the island would have been very nearly square.

East of Glastonbury lies the Sea-Goat Capricorn. Originally, his horns must have been the ridge that runs a little south of west toward the Isle of Avalon, a long narrow ridge which appears when we study the fifty-feet contour lines closely. Ponter's Ball, the currently accepted and artificially constructed horn of Capricorn looks like an afterthought, perhaps after the tides no longer came in so far and the low-lying land was dry. On the other hand, in the days when the tides did come in around that area, Ponter's Ball would have extended across the narrow part of the Sea-Goat's horns, out into the water, and would have formed a serviceable jetty on either side of the peninsula. In other words, there may have been some practical purpose for Ponter's Ball.

Looking at the Sea-Goat after all the area in his vicinity below the fifty-feet contour line has been coloured blue to represent the possible extent of high-tide water, it is both amazing and amusing to find that his long fish's tail, forefeet and head, would have vanished under the water at high-tide. Only his back and horns would have remained visible. Truly, Capricorn would have been a Sea-Goat, then, romping in the waters, but not entirely submerging himself.

Going back around the circle to the area near the Ship, and just south of that figure, we come to the Griffon. The Griffon would have presented interest at the time of high-tide, too. The rising water would have neatly cut off his head!

In recent years a veritable network of zodiacal circles have been found in Britain. For instance, in 1948 Lewis Edwards discovered the Pumpsaint Zodiac in Wales. At least three other zodiacs have been attested for in Co. Durham, and one each in Buckinghamshire, Cheshire and Essex. There are many others.

A great deal of research is now in progress. All these areas are very powerful magnetic centres. It will be interesting to find out how these zodiacs interlock with each other. We may be on the verge of a tremendous break-through in regard to our knowledge of antediluvian times.

3. The Dragon King

A separate culture might flourish here without contamination from the outside world. – *Conway*

Most people in these times regard King Arthur either as a completely legendary figure, or perhaps, as partly legendary and partly as a historical person. A few people have advanced the possibility that there were two King Arthurs, one a mystical character around whom medieval writers have woven the romantic stories that have come down the centuries to us today, and the other the more factual, less romantic king who helped to fight off the Roman invasion of Britain. However, I would like to present evidence which indicates that there was not just one, or even two, but a complete line of Arthurs!

Mrs Maltwood, referring to the Dove and the polar constellation now called Ursa Major, or the Great Bear, quotes W. T. Olcott in *Star Lore of all Ages*:

'The Northern sky is in reality a great clock dial over which hands wrought of stars trace their way unceasingly. Moreover it is a timepiece that is absolutely accurate.'

Mrs Maltwood added, 'The Great Plough appears to revolve round the heavens once in twenty-four hours, though it is the Earth that is really turning. He gives us in this chapter the other names of this constellation.

'In Ireland it was "King Arthur's Chariot", and the Druids so name it. The French called it the "Great Chariot", and "David's Chariot", which is interesting, for the effigy bird appeared to hold the Old Vicarage at Barton St David, with the church and Cross of St David in its beak.

'In the Middle Ages, in different countries, Ursa Major was known as the "Chariot of Elias", "Thor's Waggon", "Waggon of Odin", "Car of Osiris", "the abode of the Seven Sages who entered the Ark with Minos", "the waggon of Our Saviour", and "The Brood Hen".

'To sum up, the constellation of The Great Bear or Plough

was held to be the fiery Brood Hen, and appears to have carried Osiris, Minos, David, Elias, King Arthur, Thor, Odin and Our Saviour endlessly round the starry heavens every twenty-four hours.

'The Welsh Bard sings:

' "I have presided in a toilsome chair, over the circle of Sidin – the circle of the Zodiac – whilst that is continually revolving between three elements: is it not a wonder to the world that men are not enlightened."

'It is "a wonder that men are not enlightened" considering that it has always been known that the Priests of the Mysteries imitated the motions of the celestial bodies, and that they took the names of the constellations and dressed to represent the zodiacal creatures. The theology they taught was purely astronomical.

'Ursa Major contains the oldest star symbol, i.e., the fiery wheel or cross called the Swastika: it might be suggested in the circumstances that the name of the county of Somerset once had the same meaning which is familiar to us in "turning a Somersault or Somerset", for the *High History*, Branch 6, Title 11 says: "the car that the damsel leadeth after her signifieth the wheel of fortune"; this sign is represented on early British coins, and is a "symbol of the goddess of the silver wheel who guarded the limits of the British temple".

'Beside the wheel on these coins "the point within the circle" is shown, and also the trefoil or triad, with the horse of the sun.'[22]

Let us take a long look at these symbols and their references, and consider how they link together and what their linkage can reveal.

First, the list of occupants of the chariot, waggon, or car is most impressive, and shows clearly one underlying idea that was not only widespread but which covered many centuries of time without changing the essential character. Within several of the world's great religious systems this waggon or chariot drew a presiding god or some very important personage who was in some way *in direct contact* with the Divine side of things.

All these personages are in some manner or other associated with the administration on Earth of Divine Wisdom

47

or rule. In other words, it is the chariot of the Earthly member of the Twin system universally credited with organising the affairs of the human race on this planet.

This holds true even down to the last of those great ones credited with riding round and round the celestial pole in this remarkable vehicle: Our Saviour. As earthly counterpart and representative of the Father, the application becomes inevitable, and is, of course, quite correct.

This is not to say that we evaluate all members of the list as equal in any way to Our Saviour. On the other hand, each one of those mentioned performed, to some degree, the function of Divine Administrator of the affairs of mankind, and was therefore, in some way a saviour or preserver who instituted or perpetuated the Divine injunctions. It is this function that links all the great passengers in this most sacredly symbolic chariot, and which points them all out as representing the Earthly member of the original Twin system.

We must not, then, fall into the over-simplification of thinking of the Heavenly Twins as being any two definite people. *Rather, they are two offices or positions.* In early times there must have been, at any given period, one individual in each category who was 'King Paramount'. This would have been a matter of organisation. However, in each era and in every country where we come upon the symbol, we will find a hierarchy of Arthurs, and it is well known that the Divine Pharaohs in Egypt were called the Osiris.

In the quotation from the *High History*, concerning the damsel and the car, we find a reference to that ancient Atlantean book, the *Tarot*.[23] The Wheel, of Fortune, is the tenth Major Trump, and on that wheel is depicted a sphinx, which connects the damsel of the *High History* with the zodiacal sign of Virgo, the sphinx being the combined form of the two signs Virgo, the Virgin, and Leo, the Lion, and marking the epoch at which the Atlantean civilisation reached great heights in both its development and its expansion around the world.

There is, for us, an interesting connection here between two of the names bestowed upon this constellation and King Arthur, or The Arthur, as we would prefer to call the Office.

These two names are 'The Great Bear' and 'The Great Plough'. Arthur, by derivation, means 'Chief of the Bear People', and there is a legend applied to at least one of the Arthurs that when the Druids came to fetch him to become King, he was ploughing in a field with oxen.

John Whitehead, discussing the word *Arwiragus*, wrote: 'The Gaelic-Pict name it represents appears to be *Arc-wyr-auc*, Ar'wirane, "The Bear-Folk chief". The Gaelic "c" could become "t" in Pictish, both aspirated, giving *Arth-wyr*, "The Arthur".'[24]

This Arwiragus, or Arthur, was an historical figure who lived at the time of Jesus, and was his cousin, according to Whitehead, who presented chapter and verse in the form of a genealogical table.[25] Through this bearer of the title comes the connection of Glastonbury with the Grail.

Whitehead further says: 'King Arthur in the flesh thus emerges as the historical figure of "Caractacus" the Roman mispronunciation of Caratacos; or the modern Welsh Caradoc. Arthur was a tribal nickname, the British Arto – and Welsh Arthur, "the Bear" . . .' and on the next page he continues: 'Thus, although Caractacus was known to the Romans commonly by that name, he was known to the Britains by another, *Arwirauc*, which it so happens is mentioned by Juvenal in its Roman spelling *Arviragus*. The proper spelling is of some consequence, because it is clear from a manuscript in the College of Arms (L.14.ii) that the pronunciation was with a "w" not a "v"; the latter is pure misapprehension and misleading. For, *Arwir* represents the British attempt to sound the Gaelic *Arquhir*, just as in old Scots the English *when* is written quhen; the sound is not so much a different letter as merely a guttural breathing. This sound in Pictish became a dental breathing, hence *Arthwir*. Thus *Ar'wir* and *Arthur* are the same, "the Bear Folk", with the one having "-auc" added as a designation of the chief.'[26]

This connection of the Arthur with the Bear brings up some symbolic ideas. Since very ancient times and, in many countries and cultures, Ursa Major, the Great Bear, has been associated with wisdom and those who came to teach it. In India the seven stars of this constellation are known as the seven Rishis or sages. It is from the four quadrated positions of this constellation that the Swastika, emblem of divine power, is said to be derived.

Madame Blavatsky quoted Gerald Massey as saying: 'The first form of the mystical seven was seen to be figured in heaven, by the seven large stars of the Great Bear, the constellation assigned by the Egyptians to the Mother of Time, and of the seven Elemental Powers.'[27]

The Little Bear carries the Pole Star at the end of its tail. The Great Bear turns round and round the pole making a kind of clock in the sky from which both the time of night and the time of year can be determined. The association of The Arthurs with Cosmic Time, The Heavens, and the Stars, is another indication of the connection of Avalon with the Zodiac, and with 'The Heavens' in general, and, we presume, the inhabitants thereof.

Now, the Great Bear was referred to as the oldest genetrix, the Great Mother herself. Again Blavatsky quotes from Gerald Massey, discussing the Circle and the Cross:

'The four-armed cross is simply the cross of the four quarters but the cross-sign is not always simple. This is a type that was developed from an identifiable beginning, which was adapted to the expression of various ideas afterwards. The most sacred cross of Egypt that was carried in the hands of the Gods, the Pharaohs, and the mummied dead is the Ankh, the sign of life, the living, an oath, the covenant. . . . The top of this is the hieroglyphic Ru set upright on the Tau-cross. The Ru is the door, gate, mouth, the place of outlet. This denotes the *birthplace* in the northern quarter of the heavens, from which the sun is reborn. Hence the *Ru of the Ankh-sign is the feminine type of the birthplace representing the north*. It was in the northern quarter that the Goddess of the Seven Stars, called the "Mother of the Revolutions" gave birth to time in the earliest cycle of the year. The first sign of this primordial circle and cycle made in heaven is the earliest shape of the Ankh-cross, a mere loop which contains both a circle and the cross in one image. This loop or noose is carried in front of the oldest genetrix, Typhon of the Great Bear, as her *Ark*, the ideograph of *a period, an ending, a time*, shown to mean one revolution. This, then, represents the circle made in the northern heaven by the Great Bear which constituted the earliest year of time, from which fact we infer that the loop of Ru of the North represents that quarter, the birthplace of time when figured as the Ru of the Ankh symbol. . . . The Rek, or Ark, was the sign of all beginning (Arche) on this account, and the Ark-tie is the cross of the North, the hind part of heaven.'[28]

If one follows the story of the Dragon King back far enough, one comes right back to the son and consort of the Great Bear, the Mother of Time, and discovers that 'Arthur' as a title covers a hierarchy of 'people of the Bear'. In this process, too, we uncover the very interesting fact that this hierarchy claims to stem from 'the eldest of the Gods' — Saturn-Jehovah-Noah himself.

Marguerite Mertens-Steinon wrote: 'Saturn is therefore the Seed-Manu (the scythe is the symbol of the reaper): He is Noah, who gathers in the symbolical Ark the suitable elements for further evolution. "As connected with Argha, the Moon, or Ark of Salvation, Noah is symbolically one with Saturn". (S.D. 2:150).'[29]

It would not be too strange if, after the sinking of Poseid, the figurative symbol of the Ark would be adopted to represent the work of rehabilitation undertaken by the Sky People, in conjunction with those inhabitants of the earth whom they could teach the art of administration and who could become far-travelling teachers of other men.

On the same page Mertens-Steinon continued: 'Sabaoth (who is Saturn and Shiva) or the "Lord of Hosts (tsabaoth) literally means *army of the ship*, or *the crew*, or a *naval host*, the sky being metaphorically referred to as the "Upper Ocean" in the doctrine of the Chaldean Sabaeans.'[30]

This is very interesting indeed!

On another page she stated: 'We have seen that Saturn is a Cosmic God, but he is also said to be especially the "God of the Earth" . . .'[31]

And, 'All this shows that the Host of Saturn is all inclusive: we shall therefore not wonder at Saturn being called "the earliest and the last", nor at hearing that the Orphics called him "The Once," or "The Once Beyond", and Jupiter, his son, "the One", as being the Father of the Solar System.'[32]

In view of the fact that Arthur was referred to as *The Once and future King*', it is one more coincidence of note that the Orphics called Saturn 'The Once'.

Let us listen to Mertens-Steinon again. 'The sign Makara (Capricorn) is of a double nature: the pentagon or the five-pointed star, has its point turned upward or downward. This duality, to which we shall refer again in the course of this study, is well marked in the Hindu, Egyptian, and Greek zodiacal symbol of Capricorn: an amphibious animal having the front part of a goat with the body and tail of a fish – a spiritual and terrestrial symbol. The word Makara, connected with the number 5, is related to the Four Kumaras, who are 5, one being secret; to the 5 crocodiles in the celestial Nile; to the 5th hierarchy, and also to the 5th class of demons of whom Satan (Saturn as Pan), leader of the opposition in Hell, is the head. . . .

'The word Makara contains also Kama and Mara, and Saturn is related to those two Gods.

' "Mara is the God of Darkness, the Fallen One, and Death" (as the Destroyer, Saturn is the God of Death) "(death of every physical thing truly: but Mara is also the unconscious quickener of the birth of the spiritual) – and yet it is one of the names of Kama the First God in the Vedas, the Logos, from whom have sprung the Kumaras" (the Logos being Brahma-Rudra) "and this connects them still more with our 'fabulous' Indian Makara and the crocodile-headed God in Egypt." (Sebeck or Seveck who is Saturn). The word Makara is often translated by "crocodile".'[33]

It is of particular interest to note that the pentagon or the five-pointed star associated with Makara 'has its point turned upward or downward' – in other words, the star is reflected. An image of the star is suggested here. And, where do we find an image not of just one star, but of the entire heavens? In the grand zodiac in Somerset, and we find it intimately connected with 'Arthurian' legend, which brings us straight back to Saturn, or Cronus, eldest of the Gods 'who was brought in chains to Britain' – or who, as we prefer to say, was sent 'back to the land from which he was taken'. Maltwood quotes Plutarch when he wrote of Britain: 'Moreover, there is, they said, an island in which Cronus is imprisoned, with Briareus keeping guard over him as he sleeps; for, as they put it, sleep is the bond forged for Cronus. They add that around him are many divinities, his henchmen and attendants.'[34]

The zodiac, quite obviously, is pre-eminently the greatest and best symbol of Time, measured and measurable. Thus, the Somerset Zodiac would be, quite naturally, the earthly home of Time.

It can be seen that the dragon symbol is connected with both Egypt and India, and in both countries the symbol is associated with the divine representative of Time, Saturn, 'Father of the Gods'. And the gods, of course, are intimately connected with the zodiacal constellations, delineated on a grand scale in Somerset, and carried from that central Temple to the far corners of the Earth.

It would also appear to be more than mere coincidence that Makara-Crocodile-Dragon in its connection with Saturn would parallel the dragon connections of the line of Arthurs. This is all very interesting when we think of the Arthurs, or even if we happen to be orthodox and prefer to think of only one Arthur, son of Uther Pen-Dragon. However, if we choose to be unorthodox and pursue our free associations further, what comes to the mind that decides to associate Arthurs with Dragons?

Arthur, in some legends, was delivered up from the sea into the hands of Merlin by a Dragon Ship, which afterwards sailed away again, into the sky, or thin air, and nobody saw it go. Pen-Dragon must mean something. Uther Pen-Dragon was Arthur's earthly Father.

M. Oldfield Howey wrote: 'But occasionally such vessels came to Britain on other missions than conquests and destruction.

> '. . . A ship, the shape thereof
>   A Dragon wing'd.'
>   ('Coming of Arthur')

was said to have brought the good King Arthur as a babe to British shores and then to have mysteriously vanished, leaving the child to be washed by the waves to Merlin's feet.

'And the form of this fairy ship, as we all know from

Tennyson's "Idylls" was adopted by King Arthur as his ensign: the golden dragon of Britain:

> 'The Dragon of the great Pendragonship,
> That crown'd the state pavillion of the king.'

and shed its glorious rays upon Arthur's helmet as he rode into his last battle,

> 'making all the night a stream of fire.'

' "The dread Pendragon, Britain's King of Kings", was easily found by those who sought him among the throng at Camelot.

> 'Since to his crown the golden dragon clung,
> And down his robe the dragon writhed in gold,
> And from the carven-work behind him crept
> Two dragons gilded, sloping down to make
> Arms for his chair, while all the rest of them
> Thro' knots and loops and folds innumerable
> Fled ever thro' the woodwork, till they found
> The new design wherein they lost themselves.'
>
> ('Lancelot and Elaine.')

'To Arthur was assigned a celestial and miraculous parentage from Uthyr Pendragon (Head of the Dragon). Uthyr himself was the Celtic Jupiter, who, under the form of a cloud became the father of Arthur – the Celtic Hercules. Arthur's own name was bestowed on two constellations – Arthur's Chariot, now known as the Great Bear, and Arthur's Lyre.

'Gradually in the Celtic people, as in the Grecian, an unfortunate tendency arose to explain the earlier myths, the meanings of which had become obscure, by supposing they were accounts of adultery and incest. So the Uther Pendragon of the Round Table is a real Jupiter. The cloud became a human man, and the whole legend suffered degradation. . . .'[35]

Things get even more interesting and the plot thickens as

we bring in the astrological horizons so closely associated with the Glastonbury area. The nostril of the dragon turns out to be the Isle of Avalon, in the Somerset Zodiac, the place to which the fable consigns the disappearance of Arthur. (Did the dragon *breathe in*, and take back its own?) Also, for astrologers, it would seem to be of no little moment that the Isle of Avalon, in the Somerset Zodiac, represents the Air sign of Aquarius. That an Air sign should appear in a nostril would be elementary logic almost anywhere.

This particular Air sign, however, presents another curious facet, and one that is intimately connected with the Arthurian legends. In the ancient times when the Somerset Zodiac was erected, the sign of Aquarius was not represented as it is now by a man with a water jar.

Mrs Maltwood discovered that the people who erected the Temple of the Stars understood this sign under quite a different symbol, *and that symbol was the Phoenix* – the mythical bird who, at the close of its life cycle, immolated itself and rose again renewed from its own ashes! And it is this Phoenix bird, from whom we dare to believe the Phoenicians derived the name of the king from whom they claimed to be descended, that the 'intolerably' ancient architects of this primeval zodiac chose to be their representative figure of the eleventh sign.

It is somewhat of a mystery that Aquarius in modern zodiacs should be an Air sign when so little of its symbology can be traced directly to the element of Air. In modern dress, Aquarius is a man who bears a jug of water, out of which he pours and pours. Yet he is called an Air sign. He belongs indisputably to the triad of Air and so many of the events and developments that have taken place in the world since the inception of his influence (about 1750) have borne silent witness to his legitimacy.

Whenever such a discrepancy appears in a traditional sequence it denotes to the scholar, the passage of much time. The modern symbolic Aquarius, then, must not be an impostor but a development, in the same traditional way the Hercules of the Greeks was a development and great-grandson of the original Arthurs of the Somerset Zodiac, and, even farther back than that, Atlantis.

On the face of it, then, we must accept the more relevant symbol as being the older. In this case the symbol is more relevant to the air. It is a bird. Not only is it a bird, but it is a particular kind of bird – one with peculiar abilities with regard to life. *It resurrects itself.*

It is yet another coincidence to note that there is, toward the middle of the Somerset Zodiac, the figure of another bird. Its breast and part of its tail are outlined – believe it or not – by Gosling Street! It is well known that Seb, the Egyptian Goose-God, like Saturn, is referred to as The Father of the Gods, a symbol of Time and God of the Earth. And, the Orphics say, 'he (Saturn) separated his Kingdom from that of Heaven his father . . .' If we take this statement and 'play it back' to the original events and circumstances that underlie it we come, at the very least, to the basic fact that there were *two* kingdoms, one of Heaven and one of Earth. Secondly, that at one time they were not separated, but were as one. Thirdly, that it was through the Saturn (Arthurian Dragon) hierarchy that they became differentiated. That this was entirely as it should be is not mentioned, but it is implied in the surrounding legends.

All of this becomes much more practical and acceptable if we remember only one very vital point in connection with the so-called gods. It is a small point, and one that is either taken for granted or overlooked entirely. It is this: that in the beginning gods (and heroes, and demi-gods) *were actual, living people.* The first worship was ancestor worship, and no matter what sort of expanded and cosmic aspect enhaloes any god after centuries of philosophising and interpretation, that god was, in his beginning, a real, living, breathing *ancestor.* Man does not create gods in his own image. To do so would be both illogical and inane. What man does do, however, is to deify his forebears. He reveres his ancestors and those beings who taught them to be great, and he weaves his philosophy, his understanding of himself and the cosmos, around the figures of those Men the race cannot forget.

The old religion which held out in Britain until well into Christian times was referred to by its symbol the White Hart, the man with the horns, and sometimes, even the head of a hart being the male symbol of the religion. Part of the practices of this old religion which seemingly goes back at least to the caves, for we see pictures of its rituals among their paintings, and may go back to Atlantis, was the marriage of this hart-man with the Great Mother. And the Great Mother, being of the North or the 'hind' part of Heaven, as Massey points out, took on the symbol of a doe, or hind, through a magical play on words. But she was variously symbolised in different parts of the world as a She-Bear, The Moon, a Cow, and finally, we find her disguised as the mother of a god and taken up bodily into Heaven. Here religion comes full cycle by confusing the Mother with the old first sign of the zodiac, Virgo, the Virgin.

That the People of the Bear were hereditary priests of the Great Mother can hardly be doubted, and The Arthur, Chief of the Bear Folk, would have been the principal holder of the ancient traditions and put in charge of keeping the holy places – and highest among those holy places would have been the Round Table of the Zodiac in Somerset. He would be guardian of Time, or History, and also of future Time, or History-to-come, in his character of preserver of the meanings.

And so we find Time, and History, a beginning, an end, and the Mother of Time entwined with the Chief of the People of the Bear, the Zodiac, and the Temple of the Stars.

Mars was not originally associated with war. The warriors simply adopted Mars as their tutelary to whitewash their own activities. When the warriors wish to put their occupation in a good light they refer to themselves as 'guardians'. That is why they adopted Mars, who was originally the Guardian (in the sense of Sage or Yogin) of the Solar System, as their symbolic 'divinity'. Thus, Mars was in no way connected with war until the warriors themselves established this (spurious) connection in order to justify themselves and to inflate their own egos. The original 'sword' was the sword of wisdom, the 'Sword coming out of the mouth' of the Great Angel in Revelations. The warriors came along and degraded it into the sword of conquest and battle, in which form it now appears, the iron sword of the black age of iron and sorrow, the Kali Yuga.

When the Iron Age – Kali Yuga – began, the Sky People stopped coming openly to Earth, and thus we find Arthur, the Chief of the People of the Bear, drawing a sword out of a stone into which it had been plunged and where it was immobilised and useless – the stone being symbolic of the chemical world. Excalibur, then, is the sword of wisdom, the Martian-Michael 'weapon of the word', to which Arthur proves his right . . . a right he had received through inheritance and held by virtue of his Chieftainship of the People of the Bear.

These People of the Bear would have been hereditary historians and keepers of the ancient Atlantean traditional knowledge of the past and prophecies of the future. In this sense, as well as that of an actual return, an Arthur could be called 'a once and future king'.

The last of the great line of Arthurs was contemporary with Jesus of Nazareth and was related to him by blood. Whitehead has done a splendid service to the history of the world by carefully researching and presenting to all scholars a painstaking but entirely human and delightful account of the life of this great king. After the time of this Arthur there were no more. The Druids were driven into retirement and the established Old Religion collapsed into the symbology of Christianity. This was in keeping with natural progress from one Zodiacal Age to another. Old forms must perish in order that the life may continue on beyond them, keeping step with human progress and with the cyclic necessities of evolution. As the human body grows from its birth to its maturity, so the mind of man grows, too. Occasionally, it needs a new suit of clothes, a better outward form, to cope with its changing needs and occupation.

And so it was that Joseph of Arimathea brought back to the ancient holy place the relics and newborn religion of Jesus, who had been his nephew and The Arthur's cousin.

What John Whitehead does not say in his book, was that the last act, practically, of the Druids was their masterpiece of general obfuscation. Hidden meaning and obscurity mark all Druidical utterances and acts. Originally, the purpose of speaking obliquely was not to conceal but to reveal. A perfectly direct statement, if it is carefully made, can have but one equally direct meaning. However, many levels of meaning were meant to be conveyed by a Druidical utterance. Such a statement was not intended to convey merely one small segment of an idea. It was intended to be a light and to awaken the listening mind – a fire of truth to melt apparently unrelated ideas together into a comprehensive and comprehended whole.

Therefore, the idea of a hidden meaning in Druidical terms is a misnomer and no more nor less than the product of our own misunderstanding of the original intentions and purposes of the Druids. They were not, as is commonly supposed, a priesthood. They were law-makers as well as men of learning, knowledge and wisdom. But, it should be repeated, they were not priests or intercessors between humanity and God. The Druids were given the names of birds. Some were known as 'Eagles'. Others were styled 'Ravens', 'Finches', 'Swallows', and so on.

It is interesting to recall that it was the tradition of the Druids to convene their meetings at night. This tradition still holds good in our present times when the British Houses of Parliament often sit all night debating new laws or Bills.

When it became apparent that Rome and the Romans would some day, and soon, come to Britain to stamp out any surviving associations with the past, traditions that might conceivably threaten their power and the expansion of their Empire in the world, the Druids conceived of a magnificent plan to thwart Rome! The scale and magnitude of the idea seems breath-taking to us now, and in this modern day and age of easy over-communication it would not be possible. However, in the time of Claudius and the last of the great Arthurs, it was not only possible, but all the available evidence points to its having been brought off most successfully, to the entire confusion of the Roman Legions. Unfortunately, historians who have relied heavily upon subsequent Roman propaganda for their material have been confused as well.

What the Druids apparently set out to do, and apparently accomplished, was the most unlikely project of literally moving a whole 'country'. They did not, of course, dig up the soil and transport it all from one place to another. What they did do, however, was as effective, in its own way, as the impossible feat of bodily removal. They moved a kingdom.

From the original site in Somerset, contemporary place-names were applied to towns, rivers and areas much farther east. The Romans, who in their general bigotry, were not too enquiring anyway, certainly not at the military level, were taken in.

The Druids, being great students of human affairs and human ways, had an ability to predict the future to some degree. They were accomplished psychologists, and they were able to recognise probabilities of human reaction and behaviour. Therefore, they would have had time to do all this. The shift would have included moving the centre of the tin trade from Cornwall to the Isle of Wight, and a cutting off of communication between the outside world and the Glastonbury area, *thus effectually masking the existence of the holy places* in a manner entirely typical of Druidic thinking and practice.

A few years in advance of the expected occupation it would have been necessary to transport The Arthur, his family and his court, together with relatively few of the better educated and more intelligent citizens to the new area. Roman snobbery would then do the rest. If the Romans could be convinced that certain place-names agreed with those they had been sent to take and to subdue, they would then feel that their mission had been accomplished. The real places, with all they held of their traditional associations with that religion and history Rome hoped to obliterate, would have, to all intents and purposes, disappeared.

When the Druids finally made their 'last stand' against the advancing Roman Legions, marching up and down the opposite river-bank, waving branches and chanting, they must have looked quite as ineffectual and silly as they no doubt intended to appear. Unless one agrees with the Roman propaganda that came after all this, that the Druids were no more than a superstitious and pretentious lot of charlatans, suspicion arises that this puerile activity must have been another well-calculated ruse. It set the Roman minds at rest. Obviously, the Druids had been pursued to the very boundaries of their 'sacred' country, and having been driven across its borders, had summoned up their most potent spells and magic. When these apparently failed, they retreated westward. The Romans were satisfied. History tells us the Romans penetrated the western country, but it is doubtful that they realised where they were. They made no effort to obliterate the sacred effigies, and this they most certainly would have done under the circumstances, had they been able to recognise them. By acting the fool and giving the Roman Legions the sort of performance expected by the invaders, the Druids effectively preserved their most ancient and revered of Temples, with its surrounding Kingdom of Light.

When Joseph of Arimathea succeeded in giving the area a Christian gloss, the survival of the essences was assured. And so it has come down to be discovered for us in Elizabethan times by Dr Dee, and brought to light again by Mrs Maltwood in our own age. It was Mrs Maltwood who, with her air photographs and painstaking diagrams, together with maps, has furnished the key with which to unlock the carefully buried mystery.

If it seems strange and unbelievable that an assembly of Druids, marching up and down a river-bank, waving branches and chanting, could have convinced the Roman Legions that they had, indeed, driven a superstitious and after all, inconsequential, people to their extremity, it is only because we, as moderns, are out of touch with those times. The Roman soldiers had no real desire of their own to invade Britain. On the whole, soldiers go where they are told to go, and very often they do not want to go there, wherever it may be.

Confirmation of the lack of enthusiasm in the enterprise is given by Whitehead. 'So when the critical moment arrived, the Roman soldiery refused to embark. They would sail anywhere in the world, they said, but not outside it, making clever use of the late Emperor's description of Britain as "beyond the confines of Ocean" as an excuse for evading the hazardous task.'[36] It was only when Claudius sent his favourite freed slave, a eunuch called 'Narcissus', that any action was undertaken by the invading force. The Imperial representative was greeted by shouts of 'pansy', but when he declared that he would himself lead them to Britain, this was too much for the Roman Legions who at once demanded to embark on the ships of the fleet waiting to take them to Britain.

Prior to the reign of Claudius, the Roman Emperor, Caligula, had made his preparations in AD 40, for the invasion of Britain. His army had massed over the Channel at Boulogne, but the threat never materialised. Two years later, in the time of Claudius, a Roman army was once again collected at Boulogne and Arthur was making preparations to defend this Island. These constant Roman threats of invasion and continuous preparations on both sides of the Channel are very reminiscent of Hitler's massing of a gigantic invasion force on the French coast during World War II, together with counter-measures of defence in Britain under the leadership and guidance of that wise old 'bird', Winston Churchill.

By the time the Romans actually arrived in force, they would be met on unhallowed ground, but they could be given to believe they were attacking the citadel of Druidic faith and learning – and all the while, the real place, Somerset, would be 'hidden away' as thoroughly, for all practical purposes, as if it had been wiped off the face of the earth. Only those 'in the know' would be in possession of all the real facts – people like Joseph of Arimathea who went to the real Avalon – and foreigners, like the Romans, would be met with a puzzling and possibly most frustrating confusion, which better than force of arms, would provide protection for the traditionally sacred area.

And so it was that the old religion of Atlantis, the theology of the stars, came, finally, to be driven underground, quite literally, and left to the keeping of the Giant Effigies of that Temple 'builded without the sound of hammers' in the land and Kingdom of Logres, the Great Zodiac of Somerset.

Of course, the Romans did get to Somerset, built villas, and metalled the British roads, but the 'old birds' succeeded in keeping most of the Roman effort concentrated much farther east.

4. Leys and Dragon Paths

I see at a great distance, a new world stirring in the ruins, stirring clumsily but in hopefulness, seeking its lost and legendary treasures. – The High Lama

We have already discussed the importance and significance of the connection between many places of antiquity such as the Great Pyramid at Giza, Stonehenge, Avebury, The Temple of the Stars in Somerset, and the far-off Gate of the Sun at Tiahuanaco, 12,000 feet up in the high Andes on the borders of Peru and Bolivia.

All these ancient sites were chosen by the Builders because they were localities of high magnetic energy. It is now becoming increasingly evident that all these ancient places and many others all over the world are linked by lines of energy called Leys or 'Dragon Paths'. We are on the way to the rediscovery of a lost knowledge utilised by the gods who walked our earth aeons ago.

How did this re-discovery come about? The first steps were taken some thirty years ago by an amateur archaeologist who knew nothing about flying saucers (unidentified flying objects). Back in the 1920s, Mr Alfred Watkins, a well-respected merchant in Herefordshire, wrote two books, *Early British Trackways*, and *The Old Straight Track*, describing his discoveries of straight tracks or lines across the whole country, linked by standing stones, mounds, beacons, clumps of trees and crosses. These tracks were in exact alignment. Watkins called them 'Leys'. I think that the name Ley came about from the old saying 'taking the lay of the land'. As another writer, John Michell, has pointed out, Watkins, 'suddenly, in a flash saw something which no one in England had seen for thousands of years.'

At first Watkins thought that these were tracks used by the ancient Britons before the Romans came and built their roads in England. That they were used by the old tin traders from

Cornwall and others. However, later on, he changed his view on this.[37] You see, the lines were so direct and, in many instances, went straight over hill tops.

All this must seem quite incredible to most of us living in our mundane era of motorways, but the evidence that Alfred Watkins produced of these ancient straight tracks is there for all to see, supported by numerous photographs which he took himself.

More recently, Jimmy Goddard formed a Ley Hunter's Club and did considerable work mapping out additional Leys. This club has been dissolved. Now, there is a magazine called *The Ley Hunter*, edited by Paul Screeton, carrying on research into Leys and publishing articles about the latest developments.

It is interesting that many of the UFOs reported in the last two decades have been seen to be flying along these Leys. A sleepy old town called Warminster in Wiltshire, which has a very ancient history, has been the centre of a great deal of UFO activity in recent years, and it is significant that *fourteen* Leys intersect there!

The work on this fascinating subject of Leys has been taken further by the researches of John Michell. In his books he has written about the Dragon Paths, or *Lung-mei*, that have been known to exist in China for millennia. Michell points out that it is recognised in China 'that certain powerful currents, lines of magnetism, run invisible over the whole surface of the earth. The task of the geomancer was to detect these currents and interpret their influence on the land over which they passed. The magnetic force, known in China as the Dragon Current, is of two kinds, yin and yang, negative and positive, represented by the white tiger and the blue dragon. The lines of this force follow, for the most part, mountainous ridges and ranges of hills. The yang or male current takes the higher routes over steep mountains, and the yin or female flows mainly along chains of low hills. The most favoured position is where the two streams meet. . . .'

Michell also states 'In China until recently, as long ago in Britain, every building, every stone and wood, was placed in the landscape in accordance with a magic system by which the laws of mathematics and music were expressed in the geometry of the earth's surface. The striking beauty and harmony of every part of China, which all travellers have remarked, was not produced by chance. Every feature was contrived. . . .'[38]

All this means that the ancients had a magic science, including a high knowledge of the spiritual energies pervading our planet, with which we are not familiar today. Though at least a very few of us are beginning to sense a glimmering of this occult wisdom.

They had knowledge of many other things, too. For instance, Professor G. S. Hawkins proved that the ancient stone circles of Stonehenge near Amesbury were a marvellous astronomical observatory.[39]

Undoubtedly, the ancient world had a far superior civilisation to our much vaunted one. After catastrophes occurred, as described earlier, our culture and civilisation disappeared, and we now only have mysterious places like the Gate of the Sun at Tiahuanaco, Stonehenge, Avebury, Carnac in France, Baalbeck, Easter Island and a few other places to remind us of past glories. The survivors had to start all over again in a very primitive way. It is interesting that the further back you 'dig' the more sophisticated is the type of civilisation found.

John Michell's work in uncovering the 'Dragon Paths' in China and elsewhere adds to the facts advanced in our last chapter about the Dragon People.

The Dragon Paths are a remembrance of the days long ago when this planet was in open communication with people from off-planet who were known as 'The Dragon or Serpent People'.

In the last chapter we had a good deal to say about the Dragon King, and it is interesting to conjecture whether the Temple of the Stars in Somerset was also a symbolic reproduction of Arthur's legendary Round Table, with each sign of the Zodiac representing a seat for one knight. An interesting thought?

Another writer who deserves mention here is Geoffrey Ashe who has done so much good work on Arthurian research. He is co-founder and Secretary of the Camelot Research Committee, and has written several books on Arthurian themes. He has, probably, done more than any other person, today, to bring Arthur to the attention of the public. I am probably the only writer who postulates that there was a line of Arthurs, and Ashe, like those before him, only subscribes to one.

Nevertheless, in the book which he ably edited called *The Quest for Arthur's Britain*, he has done some splendid work, collecting together a team of Arthurian experts who have written on different aspects. There is interesting material on Glastonbury Abbey where the last Arthur's remains have been found. Recently, there has been a 'dig' at Cadbury, indicating that this was possibly Camelot. The book also suggested that the Isle of Avalon was at Glastonbury.

His main work has been in popularising Arthur through his books and informing us of the progress that has been made in archaeological 'digs' which have made the legendary character of Arthur more real.

I have no doubt at all that in these latter days of our present civilisation more will be discovered and revealed.

The Immortals have now left and the long line of Arthurs no longer rules our destinies. Maybe, when we understand the magic geometry and the secret science of the gods which is still here built into our ancient buildings, such as we have discussed, and even into some of our oldest ecclesiastical structures, like noble Chartres and Glastonbury Abbey, we can come to understand the eternal magic currents pervading our planet, then maybe Arthur and his knights will return. Many followers of Arthurian lore believe that this will come about one day. In Malory's words, *rex quondam rexque futurus* – the Once and Future King.

5. Rebirth of Order

Ah, but you see, we believe that to govern perfectly, it is necessary to avoid governing too much. – *Chang*

We have seen that tradition takes the office held by the line
of God-Kings, such as Neptune, Poseidon and others, going
back to Saturn-Jehovah-Noah himself. They ruled over Atlantis, and eventually, over that remaining portion of the Empire
– the 'Dry Island' – until the Roman invasion. The dual system of rulership in Atlantis was carried on in Britain, with its
two centres at Avebury and Stonehenge, the one under the
priest-King, Arthur, and a Druidic, secular lawgiver at Stonehenge.

It is not meant to be suggested that there was a continuous
line of Arthurs from Poseid to Roman Britain – probably
there was not – as the whole world was in a dire state of
upheaval and cataclysm during so much of that long time.
However, Britain, although it had its tribulations and physical
disturbances, remained on the whole above water. Poseid
went down about 9500 BC, and, it is fairly certain that for at
least 4,000 years after that life was almost unbearably hectic.
The remaining inhabitants, even those who were basically
Men in the true sense of the word, were forced by circumstances to eke out an animal-like existence, gathering their
food wherever possible.

However, memories of the Motherland, Atlantis, were to
some extent ingrained in their minds, and it was to Britain
and its survivors that the Sky People first came back on their
return to this planet. This was the first place they would pick
out from which to start the process of restoring some kind
of civilisation again on Earth. It was, after all, the Sacred
Land, 'the Dry Island', the place where the Temple of the
Stars was located. And so we see the Sky People searching
around the remnant of humankind trying to find some Men
– people whom they could rely on to pass on the fundamental

67

essentials necessary to set up some kind of social system, which would be workable and progressive. This order we know of as the Dual System of social organisation was the final product of their attempt to work out this puzzle.

After the long and gradual dissolution of the Atlantean Empire following the period of upheaval and destruction, the final sinking of Poseid removed the last vestiges of civilisation from the face of the earth. Greatly reduced in numbers, bereft of the comforts of his culture, and able to maintain only traditions that could be passed on by word of mouth to generations who eventually regarded them in the light of supernatural events, chemical-bodied earth man was reduced all over the globe, to a common level of hunter and food-gatherer. Such isolated communities as managed, somehow, to survive a little longer, like those in South America and in the Himalayan region, were themselves finally overwhelmed by the advancing chaos that had overtaken the rest of mankind.

Using the astrological cycles for a guide and correlating them with the Egyptian cycles, we find the date given by Plato for the destruction of Poseid to be accurately placed in the 'period of decline' of the Age of Leo, the Lion. At once this fact opens up a whole field of most interesting correspondences, inferences and associations.

The great zodiacal Age of the Lion lasted from a little before 11000 BC, until around 9000 BC. The destruction of Poseid, according to Plato, took place during the latter part of this period, recognisable as the cycle of decline or disintegration.

The closing centuries of the age, which are usually occupied with the renaissance of thought and discovery that marks the time of gestation of the coming new age, saw the dispersal of humanity and the migration of Atlantean mankind in all directions, eastward, westward, southward and northward. In the language of legend, the Lion could be said to have returned to the 'desert', to wander in the wilderness untamed. Man had returned to the nomadic food-gathering stage of the hunter and fisher, living in isolated family groups and settling nowhere, building no permanent shelter and following the food supply from place to place.

The mighty Lion of Atlantis had lost his Royal Heritage and had become again no more than a hunting animal. For hundreds of years he showed no sign of becoming anything else.

The Hindus say that one of the foundations of our world is a tortoise. We agree. The zodiacal sign of Cancer, the Crab, appears in the Babylonian Zodiac as a Tortoise. Both the tortoise and the crab have a peculiarity that can be applied with deep meaning to the history of mankind during this age which lasted from 9000 BC to about 6800 BC. Both crab and tortoise may be said to 'live in houses', the sea-going crab and the tortoise (a land animal), each in their shells.

The crab preserves the memory of the submergence of the last of the 'house builders', or civilised humanity. The tortoise symbolises the rediscovery of the Art of Building by those survivors who escaped the destruction of Atlantean civilisation.

It is almost a law of symbology that the older symbols tend to persist longest and when a symbol is lost or passed over, it is usually a 'Johnny-come-lately', an innovation, that disappears, and the older, more anciently historical representation is preserved and survives, albeit often brought down in time to an era nearer the present and applied to some subsequent event.

Thus, in that part of the world nearest to the location of the tragic disappearance of Atlantis, the new symbol of the Tortoise, the land-based house-builder, eventually disappeared, and the Crab, whose watery habitat preserves the memory of the fate of the lost continent as well as the suggestion of the Masonic Art, was accepted as the permanent symbol for the re-establishment of civilised life.

Meanwhile, in the East, with true colonial conservatism, the Tortoise still remains in his place among the creatures upon whose backs our present 'world' rests.

It was in the early centuries of the Age of Cancer, the centuries of reorganisation and expansion, that wandering, hunting Man – the Lion roaming in the desert – was induced to settle down. At first, he was attracted to frequent a certain spot, and finally, to erect some sort of mark of his presence there – a staff or an upright pole. Later, he built his temporary shelters around the site, and later still, his more permanent houses. The earliest known indications of such settlements are at Jarmo, about 8500 BC, and at Jericho, around 8000 BC.

What was the most prominent feature of man's first settlement in this 'New Age'? It was a spring. Water had been the destroyer. In the Age of Cancer water was to be the source of his new way of life.

We find the earliest evidences of human occupation of one site around the spring at Jarmo, and these first evidences are postholes. Archaeologists suspect these posts or poles had some specious religious significance. They base their suppositions upon observable behaviour of 'primitive' people in our own times, who erect such markers in the neighbourhood of sacred places.

Contemporary official thinking credits mankind with a spontaneous urge to frequent a certain spot and to settle there – after hundreds of millennia of the wandering, nomadic hunting life. It does not and cannot explain this abrupt change of a habit pattern believed to be as old as man himself.

We believe otherwise. Humanity is stubbornly conservative, and resists innovation unless it appears to be 'inspired'. This is particularly true of mankind in his simplest states of existence. The craze for novelty and the impetus toward change for the sake of difference is characteristic of civilised man in any age. It is a mark of unrest and rebellion, and it is not typical of man, the happy and unhappy hunter. In that stage, we contend, mankind must be taught and persuaded to do things differently.

Some of the oldest symbols in the world are embedded in the rituals of Masonry. It is agreeable to most minds that have given the matter much thought, that the oldest symbols of all are the upright pole, or the upright stone. Contemporary Freudian-orientated thought gives these earliest symbols a sexual significance. This seems unlikely in the face of observable 'primitive simplicity'. In primitive hunting family groups there is usually less emphasis on sex as a symbol than there is among civilised peoples, and such emphasis as exists is often the concern of one sex or the other (usually the female), relegated to secrecy and seclusion, and its symbols are seldom publicly displayed.

It is far more likely that man, observing himself to be the only vertical creature among a world full of horizontal quadrupeds – and, this having been called to his attention most pointedly by some more evolved creature similar to himself, but impressively advanced and capable of much he could not do – erected his marker poles and standing stones to commemorate, first of all, such visitations. Then, in the course of time, this lesson having begun to sink in, animal-man himself erected poles near places of his own frequent visitation. An upright pole, a standing stone, that advertised for all to see: *Man was here.*

The primary symbols of Masonry are Two Pillars. Not one, but two. One is coloured and one is white. Sometimes, depending upon the culture in which the symbol appears, the coloured pillar is red. Sometimes, it is black. In more developed Masonry these two pillars stand at either side of the door of a house, which, by the time of Solomon, had become a tower.

So, can we see here a commemoration of the visit to hunting man by a similar, but more evolved person (The White Pillar), their communication and the result of their conservations? We believe we do.

The first permanent shelter was probably not used continuously by earth man himself for many centuries. Erected under the direction of his Visitors, it was probably the very first religious edifice, the first temple. Before it were placed the commemoration poles. New ones were very likely added to the accumulation on the occasion of each visit to the site by Those From The Sky.

It must have been a long time, indeed, before man either dared or cared to move into such an edifice and live there himself. The desecration of the House of the Gods by such a mundane use would not immediately occur to him.

We can visualise what happened. Animal-like man is wandering about. A Sky Person (or persons) surprise a group of these almost animal men, possibly at some convenient oasis or spring. Contact is eventually established – there may have been preliminary attempts – once animal-man's inherent fear has been overcome.

And right here, the first big problem for the future of communication between the two orders is established. It has yet to be overcome after all these thousands of years. It is a problem that every human being has to resolve who encounters someone from 'Up There' – from another order of existence. Nobody can tell any large group how to solve it. This is a personal problem that each one must learn how to solve for himself, and it is this: How to keep fear from turning into awe, and sticking at that level of the emotional scale.

The other emotions fear can turn into are all characterised by the same sort of rejection inherent in fear itself. There is so much to avoid. Ever since Man decided to come back and look for his friend he has been (so to speak) walking on a tight-rope.

And Man cannot avoid it, simply because he created this necessity by involving himself with life in the chemical world in the first place.

So the Sky People set up a staff in the ground, or a stone, at the place of meeting, and say to the animal-like man: Come here again the next time the changing light (Moon) is round, and we will meet again.

Perhaps the Visitor leaves a gift before he goes. And, maybe, the contacted person only believes the marker is some kind of mysterious present.

After this sort of thing has continued for some time, the contactee learns to count, and Man says to him: After there has been a round moon for every finger of your hand, we will come again.

Possibly, it was during one of these long (to him) periods of waiting that animal-like man got the idea that if *he* brought something to the place of meeting and left it there, perhaps the Visitor could be coaxed down out of the sky a little ahead of schedule. Or, perhaps, a problem arose, and animal-man desired a piece of advice. Or, perhaps, he ate everything Man had left for him as a gift, and wanted or needed more. Whatever the cause, the act of propitiation must have been invented fairly early in the game.

When Man came back to the appointed place of meeting one day, he found gifts piled up alongside the planted staves that marked and numbered the series of his visits. Animal-man had made his first sacrifice. He had made his first offerings to the people of the sky, and had, incidentally, completed his first communication with them. Now this is very important, all of it, because it forms the basis of animal-man's religious experience, whoever and wherever he may be in the world, from the day it first happened right on down to our own present time.

No matter how elaborate the ritual, or how profound the theology involved, animal-man is still trying to coax his gods down out of the sky to help him – or, in the case of those recognised as Saints by their fellows, merely for the pleasure of their company. (This latter practice is called Mysticism, and is very highly regarded among human beings since the true Mystic is seeking no other reward – he is purely and simply 'in love with the god'. To ordinary animal-man, this appears to be most unselfish – and, therefore, almost unattainable and impractical.)

After Poseid went down, the survivors were particularly interested in coaxing help down out of the sky. It is not at all unlikely that some help came at certain times and in certain places. However, once the Sky People thought affairs on Earth looked like having a good start on their own, they tended to withdraw and to let animal-man have his freedom and his head. After all, animal-man had to learn how to handle his own proper environment in his own way. Freedom, independence and self-government, were and are his birthright in the chemical world. He must learn how to manage them for himself, to his own best advantage.

But animal-man had observed a different kind of creature. He wanted, and still wants, not only to be like that creature, but to usurp his ways (which he calls 'rights'). Animal-man is saying now, and has been saying for some thousands of years, exactly what Lucifer is credited with saying in the Courts of the Most High: I will be like God.

Man, the animal, made an obvious mistake there. He confused the people from the sky with his ideas of the supernatural, and he hasn't got that one sorted out to this day! He can't be told either. That trick was tried. A real Man was pointed out from the day of his birth – foretold, even – and when this Man grew up and tried to put over certain ideas proper to Truth, what happened to him? First of all, animal-

73

man charged him with sedition and executed him, and then, in truly Freudian reactive fashion, promoted him to Godhead.

Self-realisation cannot be conveyed by word of mouth. Or, to put it another way, you can't tell anybody anything they don't know.

So, we have the earthly brother, as Alan V. Insole points out, usurping the birthright of the heavenly [sic] or Sky Brother, and finally supplanting him, in so far as the affairs of this planet are concerned.[40] Now, the usurpers and supplanters have taken two directions of action. They have split and 'come out in two volumes' like the voice of an adolescent choir-boy. Two castes develop under these unfortunate circumstances.

Those who wish to take over the lawgiving side of animal-man's idea of his Sky Brother, become the leaders of religion and form the priesthood. In short, in these days the whole original concept of the Dual System has been completely turned over.

Those who wish to take over the administrative side of animal-man's idea of his Sky Brother – those who want earthly and temporal control of their fellow-men, become the leaders of force in action and form the armies of the world. They are the warriors. Neither the priests nor the warriors appear on earth until the Sky People have been openly here and gone away again.

Then the priests tell the people: In our trances and by our prayers and through our sacrifices (for you and sometimes of you), we get in touch with the Sky People and they speak to us. This is what they have said, and you must hear and obey.

Most of this is straight out of our sacerdotal subconscious, but never mind. They gain the power they crave, chiefly by presenting impressive ritual designed to influence the credulous – a form of mass hypnotism. And partly, at least, in our more civilised times, they win converts by promising an eternity of hell and damnation to all dissenters.

The warriors really don't care a damn about all this. They think they can see a shorter way to the enjoyment of this world's goods, powers and delights. Hurt the other fellow enough and he will give in to your demands. Kill him outright, and you can have his wife, as well as all his worldly goods and chattels – all without even asking a by your leave!

The cult of the Heavenly Twins emerged from the old Dual System of inspiration and administration begun by off-planet descendants of Atlantis who returned to rehabilitate the world. If we look at various twin-cults in different parts of the globe, and if we consider the changes that came over these cults as one religious form supplanted another down the centuries of time, we can catch dim echoes and see distorted survivals of the original system. These remnants, however, dressed up in the trappings of each time and people who saw fit to make over the old legends and traditions they could not destroy, have carried on the earthly history of mankind's revival after the tragedy of Poseid, with an amazing clarity.

Of course, it is simple, this story, once it is disinterred from all the embroidery people have hung about it in several thousand years. It is simple because it is elementary and elements are simple. There is a tendency in our complex (and complexed) time to discount simplicity. People sometimes feel that a simple, straightforward solution to a problem, or a simple, understandable, down to earth answer to a question must be rejected. Their basis for this surprising view appears to be that such a simple solution somehow reduces the magnitude of their problem, and by reflection, tends to minimise their own personal importance. This would seem to be sheer, reactive upside-down 'logic' – logic, perhaps, but logic in reverse.

Many people who set out to solve a problem find themselves engrossed in measuring it – of which pursuit there can be no end, for such attempts at measuring difficulty only serve to magnify it. So it is with the problem of the history of mankind on Earth; at least from the times of darkness immediately preceding the date 4004 BC, at which time Bishop Usher allowed the 'ecclesiastical Adam' to be created.

In order to bring mankind out of the state of intellectual and moral darkness into which he had been plunged by the final destruction of his most highly developed civilised homeland and the dispersal of its people, brethren of his from beyond the sky returned to guide and to lend a helping hand. These were his brothers, in that they could be said to be descendants of those people who, at the time of an earlier cataclysm (at that time a man-made one), had sought refuge on another planet. There they had fared better than the men who had remained here on Earth. Their problems were no longer the same as those encountered here. Their knowledge, gained through the solving of the old Earth problems, was still available to them, and there was a decision to return and to help the people who had remained on Earth toward a better way of life.

During the centuries of terrible weather that followed the Poseid disturbances (which, themselves, must have lasted for some time) the arts of agriculture and building, of husbandry, and all associated crafts were lost. Man had reverted to a primitive, food-gathering stage, and he wandered homeless, and possibly, naked in the world.

Thus, it was a vast task that the returning teachers undertook, and, it was one to be pursued slowly and cautiously, and with infinite patience. Its slow progress was logged in steps that included generations – more than one lifetime on earth for the people who were being helped and taught.

It is, by the way, probably here that the traditional idea that life on this planet 'is a school' and that we *must* return to it to 'learn our lessons' took root in the human psyche and flowered later in our esoteric philosophies. Like all such ideas it bears within it an element of truth – fundamental truth – but, on the other hand, and again like all such ideas, it has been subject to much interpretive expansion and embroidery. Mila-Repa, a Tibetan, tried to tear away some of this fancy work, and to both teach and demonstrate that 'the round of necessity' (that is, compulsive return to Earth life) was little more than a bad habit that could be broken *within one life-time*. Unfortunately, his influence failed to spread very far outside Tibet. The path of least resistance may be the easier way, but it is the long way round.

It may well be that Mila-Repa, who obtained his knowledge from a teacher who was himself one of the hierarchical line of teachers that reached back to Heavenly knowledge, was only attempting to restate in simple terms the original instructions, as they were given by those who returned from beyond the sky to open the eyes of mankind.

6. Brother Builders

I will not try to describe the association that sprang up between
the two; the one gave utmost adoration, while the other shared
his knowledge . . . – *The High Lama*

The traditional sanctity of islands remained as a concept in
the minds of many peoples long after the historical details
had collapsed into one another and faded away down the
long perspective of time.

Before we can begin to write about the use of water to
separate certain sacred areas or islands, and the significance
of these separated areas, and before we can write about
bridges, keepers of bridges, boats and boatmen, it must be
understood how the mind of Man looks at Space. The most
universal symbol for Space, for that immeasurable and primordial area within which suns burn as incandescent sparks
and where planets float like bits of dry land, or island, is a
vast and limitless ocean, a Universal Sea.

Thus, the element that best symbolises Space to the human
mind is Water. According to Genesis: 'And the earth was
without form and void: and darkness was upon the face of
the deep. And the Spirit of God moved upon the face of the
waters . . .'

The secondary meaning of water, which is Wisdom, derives
from the experience of the human race when it was taught by
people who arrived on Earth from Space (or from other
planets). When knowledge of the actual structure of the Solar
System dimmed and disappeared from Earth, humanity's
religious ideas became correspondingly limited, until now we
have mankind believing in a Heaven 'somewhere out there'
which is immaterial and partakes of the nature of Space itself.

The Hindus, however, understood the idea of islands, and
spoke in their Puranas of the 'seven islands' separated from
one another by seven oceans, surrounding and encircling the
Earth. By the time their books were written, their knowledge

had degenerated to a geocentric concept of the Solar System. Nevertheless, the island idea remained. Thus, in addition to its representing a near event in human history, the submergence of Poseid, an island has a deeper and more cosmological meaning, connected with communication with other planets, which are other islands in Space, as is our own Earth.

The priesthood appointed itself communicators with those who lived on those other islands and who occasionally brought knowledge, wisdom and learning to Earth mankind, or who were credited with having done so in the past. The priest came to be looked upon as a person who could bridge the waters, or space, existing between Earth and the dwelling-place of the people from elsewhere.

After those people withdrew and no longer came openly as they had done in the beginning, the idea grew up that they were incorporeal and spiritual entities. The priests set themselves up as being able to communicate with these entities and placed themselves in the position of transmitting laws, rules, regulations, promises and prophecies.

Certain telepathic people may have been able to do this, but there can be small doubt that most of those who formed the priesthoods of later times were only hopeful imitators, or, at least in some cases, outright pretenders. The belief that the power to communicate was transmissible led to the establishment of Holy Orders. The Pope himself is called Pontiff, from the Latin word for bridge (*pons*), because he is supposed to act as liaison between Heaven and Earth, between the Most High and Humanity.

The bridge idea appears elsewhere in the religions of mankind, notably in the Scandinavian system, where it became the Rainbow bridge, the heavenly span over which valiant warriors who died in battle were conveyed to Valhalla where they enjoyed the company of the gods.

In discussing Japanese traditional ideas of creation, Blavatsky wrote: 'The Seventh Spirit, the last emanated from the "Mother" appears as the first divine human form distinctly male and female. It was the seventh "creation" as in the Puranas, wherein man is the seventh creation of Brahma.

'These, Tsanagi-Tsanami, descended into the Universe by the Celestial Bridge, the Milky Way, and "Tsanagi, perceiving far below a chaotic mass of cloud and water, thrust his jewelled spear into the depths, and dry land appeared. Then the two separated to explore Onokoro, the newly created island-world".'[41]

Even in this modern age, as Man once again reaches out for the stars, outer Space is coming to be regarded as an ocean. Ira Wolfert, in the September, 1961, issue of the *Reader's Digest*, wrote:

'On any average day now, more than 25 satellites are travelling in outer space – an amazing fleet, sailing an amazing *ocean* on a tremendous mission of exploration.'

The italics in the above quotation are mine.

Modern scientific ideas have finally got round to a literal and sequential interpretation of Genesis, and in our times it is quite normal to speak of Space as an ocean. We always say spaceSHIP. Apparently the human mind conceives of journeys from one bit of dry land (planet) to another as voyages from one island in Space to another – hence the inevitable comparison of Space with a vast sea.

Out of this concept grew the practice of surrounding a special place with water, thus creating a sacred island – and this they did, even if they had to dig a ditch around it. It was only comparatively late in the history of this idea, when the warriors adapted current usages to their own purposes, that the moat as a part of a system of defence came into being. Before that it was a representation of the sea that surrounded the sacred place.

Also, out of this concept, boiled down and distilled from actual historical fact, came the other idea of a Temple Pool, usually with a little island in the middle, or perhaps a statue, or a fountain. Either way, it was all done in memory of (1) the Isles of the Dead (Poseid, and all the rest of the submerged Atlantean Empire), and (2) the Isles of the Blest, or the Fortunate Isles . . . telescoped, collapsed, and thought about as if they were the same. In any event, sacred, both to the dead and to the living.

At Avebury, for instance, the defence idea is clearly not connected with the moat, which is inside the earthwork, not outside it. Avebury, in Wiltshire, about five miles west of Marlborough, has a big earthwork and stone circles. An enormous, roughly circular ditch contains the remains of a great circle of originally 100 upright stones. They are all sarsen-stones, many of them very large, some weighing around forty tons. Inside this great circle, which covers an area about 1,400 feet in diameter, were two smaller stone circles.

Dr William Stukeley, the famous antiquary, who visited Avebury in the early 1720s, described 'two great serpentine avenues of this triple temple, which were such an important feature of this work and distinguished it from nearly all other Celtic temples. These avenues of approach consisted of double rows of upright stones, which branched off from the central work to the extent of more than a mile each. One of them turned off from the outer circle to the south, veering near its extremity to the south-east, where it terminated in two circular, or rather elliptical ranges of upright stones, which were on an average 86 feet apart from each other in lineal direction.

'The head of this gigantic serpent was formed by a terminating temple of two concentric ovals, of which the outer measured about 146 feet in diameter, and the inner was 45 feet across. This was placed upon a height known as Overton Hill, which forms the southern promontory of the Hakpen Hills. As "Hakpen" means "Serpent-head" there seems little doubt that the range derived its name from the temple.

'The Western avenue extended about one mile and a half, and consisted of two hundred and three stones; its extremity ending in a point, or with a single stone, to represent the tail of the serpent.

'The distance from the serpent-head promontory to the end of the serpent's tail is about two miles, whilst the area occupied is upwards of twenty-eight acres. The whole of the large circle is surrounded by a deep and wide ditch and rampart, measuring 70 or 80 feet in height from top to bottom, except where two openings corresponding to the two great avenues, were left as entrances to the temple.

'The bank is now broken in four places, but these two were probably the only original ones. About halfway up this inner slope was a sort of terrace walk apparently adapted for spectators of the sacred ceremonies.'[42]

It is interesting to note that the Department of the Environment, who are now guardians of Avebury for the National Trust, do not mention the Western Avenue in their guidebooks at all. They refer only to the avenue leading from the Outer Circle to the south, known as Kennet Avenue. It is true that no stones now remain on the Western Avenue. Indeed, a great deal of excavation and restoration has been done on Kennet Avenue since 1934 and the route of this part of the serpent has been traced back to what is known as the Sanctuary on Overton Hill, bearing out Stukeley's report.

A tremendous amount of destruction has been done at Avebury down the centuries. Stukeley described in his notes the demolition of the stones. These unhappy events were occurring during his visits to the area, although they had begun well before and continued long afterward. The guide books do credit Stukeley not only with this information but bear him out. These destructive acts to Avebury in the eighteenth century were apparently carried out by farmers and builders. At other times, the Lord of the Manor had a section of the Outer Circle stones cast into the ditch. Add to this, that many of the houses and garden walls of the village of Avebury and other local villages have been built with stones from the temple, and it can readily be seen that many difficulties have been added to the work of archaeologists in the area.

Stukeley goes on to say: 'It would be interesting to discover the name bestowed on the Great Serpent by its builders. Abury or Avebury, was written as Aubury in the ancient books of Malmesbury Abbey. This was probably a corruption of Auber, i.e., the "Serpent-sun", Aub being the Eastern name of the serpent, and aur or us, signifying light, and being a title of the sun-god. There is a remarkable artificial mound of great height, midway between the terminations of the serpentine avenues, known as Silbury Hill, i.e., the "Hill of the Sun". Its name is a further confirmation that the temple was sacred to the sun-god, and to the serpent as his symbol.

'Sir Richard Hoare has given us the measurements of this hill as calculated by Edward Crocker, a scientific practical surveyor. According to these, "The circumference of the hill as near the base as possible, measures 2,027 feet, the diameter at top, 120 feet, the sloping height 316 feet, and the perpendicular height 170 feet, but that part of our measurement which will excite the most surprise is, that this artificial hill covers the space of five acres and thirty-four perches of land."

'Sir Richard Hoare considers that there can be no doubt it was one of the component parts of the grand temple at Abury, not a sepulchre mound raised over the bones and ashes of a king or arch-druid. Its situation in opposition to the temple and nearly in the centre between the two avenues, seems in some degree to warrant that supposition.'

The Department of the Environment guide-books state that immigrants from Holland and the Rhineland known as the Beaker People arrived in England about 1700 BC, and were responsible for a goodly part of the building of Avebury, Stonehenge and many other circles and barrows. Frankly, I do not go along with this concept in its entirety. At least, not in regard to Avebury. The Beaker People certainly made certain additions and amendments – they were used to dealing with metals and were of a more evolved civilisation than the earlier Neolithic peoples – and, they too, probably carried on the ritualistic practices of the solar serpent worship in these temples. However, I would suggest that the origins of Avebury, like Carnac in Brittany, extend much farther back than the Beaker People. Indeed, I would place the birth of Avebury prior to their Neolithic predecessors.

Carnac, in Brittany, was also a great serpent temple with rows of stones winding like a great snake for about eight miles. This fantastic place has around 10,000 stones! Over 300 are more than fifteen feet in height.

Howey, in his remarkable and erudite work, quotes Dr Fresne, regarding the dragon which played a big part in the processions of the Roman Catholic Church. He wrote: 'On Palm Sunday there are two processions in which the standard and the dragon precede. Holy water and a censer without fire; a cross and dragon on a pole are borne in procession. One of the boys, however, carries a lighted candle in a lantern, that fire may be at hand in case the light which is in the dragon's mouth should be extinguished. Here it is evident that the church has preserved an ancient rite of the Ophiolaters. The sacred fire in the dragon's mouth, which so carefully was safeguarded from extinction, at once brings to mind the holy fire kept perpetually burning on the altars of the children of the sun, whilst the dragon on the pole was the standard of the serpent worshippers wherever they were to be found. The whole ceremony was probably a re-enactment of an ophite procession through the winding ways among the stones of Carnac.'[43]

Howey states that Carnac really means Cairn-hac, that is 'the Serpent's Hill, cairn meaning a mound or heap of stones, and hac being an old Celtic word for serpent. The top of it appears to be artificial, and it no doubt was the spot on which the altar was erected where the perpetual fire kindled by the sun was kept burning, as prescribed in the rites of the fire-or-sun worshippers of Persia and elsewhere.'[44]

In the Northern Sky, there are two major constellations prominent in any age. They appear to travel round and round the celestial pole and the pole of the ecliptic. These two are the Great Bear and the Dragon, Ursa Major and Draco, as we call them now.

They are always obvious because they consist of bright stars that are easily seen and associated. Over a period of many thousands of years the distribution of their stars will change, that is, they will change their apparent shape, as constellations. This is because the stars themselves are in motion, and change their positions very slowly. (This is called 'proper motion'.) One hundred thousand years hence, the Great Bear will not have the same configuration it has today, but it will still be a bright and impressive group of stars, and it will again be swinging round the north celestial pole in much the same way it does for us now.

Seventy thousand years ago, Neanderthal Man worshipped and sacrificed in a great, deep cave, high in the Alps. This cave is called the Drachenloch, and it lies near the top of a peak above the Tamina Valley, at an altitude of 8,000 feet. The pathway up to it is difficult, intricate and tortuous. In this cave there are, among other interesting things, a 'bone altar', a fire pit, and there are many bear bones, as well as the carefully preserved and often concealed skulls of bears.

A full description of these and other important finds of a

similar nature is given by Ivar Lissnar. He gives in great
detail accounts of the worship of the bear that still continues
to this day among the circumpolar peoples who have not yet
succumbed to the inroads of progress and technological civilisation. However, he comments: 'Bear cults . . . originated in
a younger subarctic culture and are found in regions further
south. . . .'[45]

By date and time, then, the Bear Cult is the oldest surviving
form of religion in the world. It belongs not merely to the
Atlantean cycle, through which it has obviously survived with
its forms, observances and rituals still marvellously intact, but
reaches back into the depths of human history on this planet.
Seventy thousand years is, of course, an approximation, but
even so it comprises almost three grand zodiacal cycles of
precession.

Seventy thousand years ago, when 'Lemurian' Man was per-
forming his Bear sacrifices, the Great Bear constellation was
making its nightly rounds, as if walking round and round the
north pole of the heavens. The pole star of that time was not
Polaris, as it is now, but one of the stars in the tail of the
constellation Draco, the great serpent or dragon, which is the
other great constellation intimately associated with the polar
sky.

Many primitive tribes that have survived until our own
times venerate these constellations, particularly the one called
the Bear. They also observe the ancient bear sacrifice, and
part of this observance involves tying a bear up to a stake or
a pole, and making the animal walk round and round – a
savage custom, we may say, but one that has its roots in some
long-past knowledge of astronomy. Mankind's religion, it has
been shown, does not originate in superstition as the evolutionists believe. As religion is the remnant of real knowledge,
so superstition is the degraded ghost of a religion that has
deteriorated.

In our own time, the people who still follow the old religion
of the bear are those who live in the comparatively undis-
turbed regions surrounding the north pole. Thus, there are to
be seen here, immediately, two factors which have contributed
to the survival of that religion: the comparative isolation of
the people from what we call progress and the advancement

of civilisation, and their location, near the pole, where the movements of the stars and the old sacred constellations are clearly visible and pronounced.

Traces of the old Bear Cult are found much farther south, however, as we have seen. In the Alps, for instance, and much more recently, we believe, in England, where the symbol of the dragon still abounds, and where we have the great secular chief who was associated with the Temple of the Stars, and whose name means Chief of the Bear People.

At any rate, the Dragon or Serpent plays a very great part in the traditions of mankind. And, we might note here, the Dragon or Great Serpent, can be seen with either one or two heads, according to the way one interprets the two stars that lie at that end of his body. The Egyptians appeared to use both symbols, the one-headed and the two-headed, to illustrate two concepts or interpretations having to do with creation and with Man.

We have been told, and read in many books, that 25,000 to 30,000 years ago there was a terrible conflict between two kinds of human inhabitants upon this earth. We can read further that the conflict was largely at the mental or emotional level, but other sources say that one kind of human being had attained a sufficiently high technology to permit at least some of its number to escape this planet and to go away to another. Be that as it may, it is most interesting to compare dates, and to discover that for some reason, about 3000 BC, Neanderthal Man disappeared rather suddenly from the face of the earth. It is not outside the bounds of possibility or plausibility that he was, to some degree, assimilated by marriage into the race of his conqueror – a race which appeared suddenly in numbers from an unknown source, and which, in its turn, died out as a pure species. Characteristics of both races, however, are still discernible now and again in people living at the present time.

What is most remarkable here is that the religious beliefs and practices should have survived for so long, and should still be alive today, and that they appear woven into our own religious and mythological heritage. That the two seven-star constellations that move round the pole star should still carry, among so many apparently divergent peoples, the names of

Great Bear and Little Bear is passing strange, and witnesses the importance attached to the old body of ideas connected with them.

Man has always liked to worship at or near the tops of mountains, and he has made small mountains (mounds) of his sacrificial objects. He has taken those objects up toward the sky as far as the earth will allow him to go, and when a mountain proved unclimbable, he has called that mountain holy. Mountains are steps toward the sky, where his gods are, and where people who are nearer, apparently, to those gods, live – and, last but not least, where certain Men of the Earth went away to live at a time when there was much death.

It would be only one short step from such a tradition to the notion that perhaps all the dead, or at least a certain number of them, went to the sky. A shaman, for instance, is still never buried in the ground. His body is always placed on an elevated platform, or up in a tree. And it is the shaman's business to go, through trance, walking in the sky and to contact the entities there.

The veneration of mountains, hills, tors and high islands is world-wide. There came a time when mankind began to build sacred mounds, some of them of great size. This, however, was a very late development.

Throughout the earliest times, certain high places, hills and mountains, were held sacred. Is it too much to suppose that the Prescelly Hills, which could be seen from so far away by travellers upon the sea, and from which came the sacred blue-stones that formed a part of Stonehenge, were one such sacred eminence? Or, that the Marlborough Downs, where the huge blocks were found that form the rest of the Stonehenge Monument, were another such holy place? The connection with sanctity would appear to be further strengthened by recent archaeological research. Albert Maisel, writing in an article, 'The Secret of Stonehenge', in the October 1961 issue of the *Reader's Digest*, reveals that it has been discovered that the stones were hauled from the downs through Avebury before being taken on to Stonehenge. Were they ceremonially consecrated there, first because they had come from a sacred spot, and second because they were on their way to another? There are other possible routes between the

Marlborough Downs and Stonehenge, yet the men who built that monument brought their material through Avebury and past the artificial sacred mound, Silbury Hill. Doubtless they had a reason.

Why did mankind venerate mountain-tops, hills and even go so far as to create special artificial ones like Silbury Hill? Those apparently sacred natural areas such as the Marlborough Downs, may have been remembered as places where, in times long ago, a few centuries after the sinking of Poseid, the Sky People came down and instructed earth man.

Not very far from Avebury, the celebrated Uffington White Horse is to be seen just under the crest of the White Horse Hill on the Berkshire Downs. Some 500 feet lower lies the well-known Vale of the White Horse. Above the famous cut figure of the horse is the ancient, circular camp called Uffington Castle, with superb views over several surrounding counties. Below this earthwork, on one side of the hill, are The Dragon's Stairs, and beyond them lies Dragon Hill, so named because Uther Pen-Dragon is supposed to have been buried there.

The Uffington White Horse has aroused more interest and curiosity, as to its origin and meaning, than any other white horse chalk figure cut on the soil of this ancient island. This is, first of all, because the carved horse is quite unlike any other. It is, the experts agree, much older than the others, but they do not agree as to the date of its origin.

Many authorities consider that Alfred caused it to be cut in commemoration of his defeat of the Danes at Ashdown in AD 871. Others, including Aubrey writing in the seventeenth century, wrote that the Uffington White Horse was cut by Hengist, the Saxon invader, who bore one on his standard. However, subsequent investigators have declared that the Uffington Horse bears a strong resemblance to horses on various early Iron Age coins. Nevertheless, there are certain differences, and the well-known modern authority on hill figures, Morris Marples, goes so far as to say that the Uffington Horse may belong to a more primitive age than that of the early Iron Age horses generally noted as parallels.[46]

The White Horse itself, as already indicated, is strangely enough, quite unlike any of the many other later horses carved in the turf of the English countryside. It is unique in its appearance, and looks more like a *dragon* than a horse. It is longer than the largest of the other horses, being 365 feet in length. In its prominent position above White Horse Vale, it can be seen for miles around – on a clear day for about fifteen to twenty miles – but best of all, it can be seen as a most outstanding landmark from the air.

If we recall the Temple of the Stars in Somerset, and again, how the effigies depicting the signs of the zodiac can best be seen from the air, then the real significance of the Uffington White Horse can be understood. It is true that the horse can be seen from the ground over a wide area, but from the air it shows up from a very, very long way off – in its true proportions. It was meant to be seen from the sky!

The White Horse, in symbology, represents Mind, the one quality that most clearly distinguishes Man from the animals. This particular white horse was pictured on White Horse Hill like a Dragon, and Uther Pen-Dragon, the Paramount Sovereign, 'King of Kings', is said to be buried nearby. Was the White Horse a sign – a symbol – to other men, Sky People? Was it a permanent landmark – a signpost – to those who came to rehabilitate this planet after the sinking of Poseid? Was the White Horse Hill area the burial ground of the Royal Line of Arthurs?

Dragon Hill is an especially big mound for a burial place, befitting such a person as Uther Pen-Dragon. There are many other burial mounds scattered around the British countryside. These are usually in the shape of what are known as Long Barrows, which, on being excavated, contain the remains of women. Bearing in mind that in those far-off days the memory of visits from the sky would still be retained in some form by the peoples of that era, is it just a coincidence that their burial mounds – long barrows and discs – should bear such a strong resemblance to the cigar-shaped and disc-shaped objects in the sky, reported to have been seen again by so many thousands of people all over the world in recent years?

These barrows are to be found in great numbers in the area around Stonehenge and Avebury. We all know, too, that in ancient times the Egyptians and others buried their rulers under great mounds, hills, and pyramids. The last of the

Arthurs, together with his consort, was believed to have been buried in Glastonbury Abbey, in Somerset. If you visit the ruins of the Abbey today, you will find a tombstone indicating the exact position of the grave, not far from the site of the High Altar. However, it should be remembered that the last of the Arthurs, the one who fought the Romans, was the son of Cymbeline. He was a true bearer of the Office of the Arthur, but he was not the son of Uther Pen-Dragon.

After the Age of Gemini, The Twins, closed, about 4700 BC, the New Age of Taurus, The Bull, began and the Sky People gradually withdrew. Their spadework for the rehabilitation of civilisation on Earth had been completed. Earth man was now left to look after himself, and the priesthood assumed the role of subsitute for the Sky People, setting themselves up as law-givers and instructors.

Doubtless, occasional visitors returned to keep an eye on human progress, and the memory of former times remained in the minds of earth people for centuries, at first as historical fact, and then as myth and legend. These would be embroidered by the dogma and interpretation the priests gave the original picture to suit their own purposes at different times.

The Sky People did not leave before earth men were well on their way toward the re-establishment of some kind of civilisation. During the Age of Cancer, certain earth people were induced to form permanent settlements. In the next age, that of Gemini, The Twins, which began early in the seventh millennium BC, through close and continued contact, a dual system of instruction and administration was introduced between the two races of mankind. The earth man selected to be administrator for any particular local area would be the secular chieftain, but no priest, since the Sky People would have been too familiar to have seemed to be supernatural. In this age, Man on Earth learned to build rectangular houses, in addition to the older domed or beehive shape. He was using thumb-pressed bricks, and plastering his floors and walls.

This could well be the time in antiquity from which it is possible to trace the first beginnings of the Craft of Masonry. It would seem so, if instruction in architecture and building

was given symbolic meaning by the sky-side. The first frater-
nal organisation of earth man in this cycle could have begun
to develop. Or, did it arrive 'full-blown'? The impression of
the thumb is surely a mark of the workman which nobody
could imitate, and a close examination of Masonic symbolism and reference reveals many other possible remains which
become all the more remarkable when one considers that the
symbology was constructed (according to common belief) and
the rituals composed during a time when little or nothing was
known of these most ancient civilisations that appeared during
the Age of the Brothers.

Is this just another interesting coincidence? Was the Master
of the Lodge – the earthly administrator – left in charge of the
instruction and the work during periods when the Sky Person
was absent from his seat (which, at rather more than a guess,
would have been placed toward the north)? And, once things
were organised and under way, did the Sky Person return
only for periodic meetings, to ensure that all was going well
and to offer further instruction and advice?

7. The Sons of Thunder

We have no jailors, save those that Nature herself has provided.
— *Chang*

That the original brothers, the Primordial Twins, were the two races of mankind involved in this endeavour would seem to be the fact underlying all the later growth of personification, legend, myth and embroidery, that has come down to us about the Twins. One was the Heaven-born race, the so-called Divine Twin. The other was the Earth-born race, the so-called Human Twin, who receives the benefits pertaining to the Heavenly Brother and who supplants him. The younger or human brother, usurps the authority of the other, Heaven-born or Heavenly brother, and sets himself up to run the whole show. Sometimes, the too ambitious student who learns a little from his teacher, suddenly feels himself to be the superior of that teacher, and launches himself into rash and reckless misuse of the little he has learned. Indeed, 'a little knowledge is a dangerous thing'.

Insole has much to say about the cults of Heavenly Twins, and what he says, considered in this new light, may take on a greater depth of meaning and a practical pertinence beyond the sphere of religion. It may reveal another lost chapter in the long history of Man.

'The Cult of the Heavenly Twins, or Sons of Thunder, was at one time widely distributed over the whole world. The acvins or Twin Horsemen are mentioned more than four hundred times in the Rig Veda. The Dioscuri, who rode horses at the Battle of Lake Regulus, as Castor and Pollux, are late stages of their development. In the first instance, we are told by Dr Rendal Harris:

' "It is better to think of them as the Great Twin Brethren, without special names or descriptions and without their horses . . . it is certain that they can be regarded as typical saviours of persons in disability and distress." '[47]

Both those who came to teach, and the first men of Earth who learned from them, would be considered, by the rest of the world, as saviours and rescuers of persons in distress. From the point of view of the distressed, these two sorts of people would be 'twins' and brothers – both would be distributing the same ideas, teaching the same arts, bringing the same gifts. From the viewpoint of the recipients of these favours, one twin would be Heavenly, that is, from the sky, and the other would be Earthly. Both would assume the role and value of heroic saviours to those who were being helped.

Insole again: 'About 2500 BC there must have been an Indo-European civilisation in an area of central Asia slowly turning into desert. Although we have discovered no traces, it must have been in some ways more advanced than the contemporary civilisations of Sumeria, Egypt and Crete, because these Indo-Europeans were the first to discover the wheel, the potter's wheel, to tame the horse and invent chariots. *It would appear* that it was in the lost civilisation that the great British symbols, Andrew with his Unicorn, Michael and George with their Red Cross, and Britannia with her helmet, trident and crossed shield, first evolved into their complex pattern.'[48]

That last sentence is very interesting. The italics are mine. 'It would appear' would seem to indicate a certain doubt in the mind of the author, and well enough it might. Take a look at the date given: 2500 BC, far too late. Therefore, it would only *appear* that the symbols evolved into their complex pattern *at that time*. And, if we accept that appearance, something else immediately appears: that they probably originated somewhere else, and at an earlier date. Why not in the very home of those symbols? Why not in the land of Britannia, Britain? It is well agreed that the Trident is an Atlantean symbol, wielded by Poseidon, Neptune, and connected with the sea. It would be odd, indeed, to find it actually originating in 'an area of central Asia slowly turning into a desert'!

But to go on with Insole:

'A second migration passed over the Hindu Kush into India about 1500 BC. They brought with them those legends of the Twins which are now incorporated in the Rig Veda,

which work – world-famous as it is – has never been fully
translated into English as it is under the puritanical taboo.

'A third wave passed across south Russia about 1100 BC.
Some settled in Macedonia, and others passed on and invaded
both Italy and Greece. These were the Dorian Greeks whose
God Zeus replaced the older Cronos, and who captured
Troy. Another indication of a lost common origin will be
found in the many similarities between the Indian Ramayan
Epic and Homer's Iliad.'[49]

Here again Insole stumbles upon but does not pick up
another important piece: Cronos is Saturn *who was sent in
chains to Britain*. The oldest of the gods, when he was displaced, was not sent into exile, as everybody has supposed –
he was sent home, back to his own temple, the Temple of
Time – the Temple of the Stars. And, this sending home of
the God of Time reflects and states the realisation by the
people of that era of the true place, the setting and the source
of all their 'divine knowledge' as surely as if it had been
written up on a cosmic sign-board for all to read.

Then Insole states: 'From Dr Rendal Harris we learn that
the Heavenly Twins were river-gods who go to sea.'[50]

The Dragon estuaries of Somerset are fed by rivers, one of
them the Parrett bearing a Phoenician name, according to
Maltwood. Ludonium, the city of Lud, God of 'Light' (which
can mean truth, knowledge, intellectual illumination), is also
on a river – the Thames – and part of the same island. If the
Light brought by the Heavenly Twin came from the 'sea',
symbolising both the lost Atlantis and Space (which last is one
of the symbols proper to the sea), then that twin could be
identified with an important and much reverenced river system. If those he taught, the Earthly Twin, built their first city
on another river, and for good, simple and sufficient reason,
chose to dedicate it to the Light they had received, then that
Earthly Twin would, for equally good reasons, be identified
with another important river, the Thames, by those who later
learned from them.

Still referring to the Heavenly Twins, Insole says:

'They first taught men to build ships, hollowed out of the
sacred oak. They protect sailors from the dangers of shallows
and of the seas. They founded the first cities. They invented

the ox-drawn plough of stone and wood. They were deities of rejuvenation, and generally promoted fertility in nature and men. They healed the sick, especially the blind. They appeared upon battle-fields as the harbingers of victory.'[51]

The more we look at this list of activities, the more it becomes apparent that we have here a catalogue of the doings of those who returned from the heavens (the sky) and those whom they first taught.

The Dual System then, is a system of rulership. It is the system of government and instruction established under the influence of the Age of Gemini, the Twins, for the guidance, development, and deliberately undertaken social evolution of animal-like Man. Under this Dual System there are two kings who are equal in rank but who are different in function. Because in some places villages are built along two sides of a single street, and the members of each moiety live on their own side of the street, we can refer to the two sides of the Dual System as 'the two sides of the street'.

Perry states: '. . . The political and social constitution of the Caroline Islands must formerly have been based upon a thorough-going dual system. Even at the present day society is organised in that way. Each village is ruled by two families, which provide respectively the sacred and war chiefs. These two families intermarry, and this rule holds good throughout the village, so that a man has to take his wife from the other group. Sometimes the village is arranged as two parallel rows of houses, with a street between, and the members of each group have to live on one side of this street. Each village, when large enough, has two landing stages, one for each side. . . .'[52]

Originally, one side consisted of a line of priests, teachers and lawgivers. On the other side were the ministers, administrators and men of commerce.

In Egypt the Dual System appeared at the very beginning of dynastic times. The two kings ruled simultaneously and each was responsible for his own sphere of duty and activity. On one side there was the Priest-King (Divine Ruler) – who later on lost his kingship and retained only his priesthood. In contemporary times, this side is represented only by religion and the hierarchy of the Church. In the old order the Divine

King and his councillors produced and preserved the body of the law, regarding social organisation, justice, customs, manners and behaviour.

The Divine King was either an extra-terrestrial or traced his descent from one. He was a Son of the Sun. The Divine King married either a woman of his own immediate family (usually his full or half sister) or a woman from the secular society (on the other side of the street).

It was recognised that descent was Matrilineal, because of his ties to Earth, since the Father of the Divine King was an extraterrestrial. Thus, in the beginning, brother and sister marriage were token unions for ceremonial purposes and symbolic reasons. Early Egyptian history has this on record. If incest occurred in these marriages it was a late development during a time when the system was degenerating. In the case of plural marriages, the son of the King's 'sister-wife' took precedence over the offspring of the secular wife or wives.

The Divine moiety venerated the Sun, the Stars, and the Sky People, as religious symbols. The Secular King married a woman of the Divine moiety, but 'on this side of the street' descent was patrilineal, again showing the ties to Earth and the connection with it. The father of the Secular King was a Man of the Earth, even though his mother may have been a woman descended from the Children of the Sun.

Thus, the worship and veneration of the Moon ('the lesser light'), the Bull (earth as energy-producer), and the Mother Goddess (earth as producer of food and form) belonged to the moiety of the Secular King. Also, the veneration of Heroes, offspring of the union of gods with human women, grew up in this moiety at a later date.

The Dual System of Social Organisation belongs 'par excellence' to the Age and sign of Gemini, the Twins. Legendary history (or 'historical legend' if you prefer) is crammed with references to sets of twins, their doings and accomplishments. This is true of any culture in the world with roots in any real antiquity. For example, see the literature of India – Egypt – the tales of the Polynesians, the American Indians, the Japanese and the Chinese. Any people, anywhere, who have preserved ancient traditions tell of these original and originating

Brothers. (One wonders if the legend of Romulus and Remus was in existence long before the foundation of Rome and was only brought down in time to apply to the building of the 'Holy City'.)

The Age of Gemini endured between approximately 6800 BC and about 4700 BC. Then began the zodiacal Age of Taurus, the Bull, the emblem of the Secular Kings. At this time, the Divine King began to lose his earthly power and significance, and during the Age of the Bull, he was finally transformed into a religious leader only, without secular power or authority. The Secular King took over the entire management of Earthly affairs, and became at the same time a Warrior King.

Of course, this transformation did not occur all at once, nor did it take place at the same time in all places throughout the world. It was a gradual process, and in some outlying areas there are still so-called 'primitive' tribes which still practise some form of the ancient dual organisation.

In fact, it is so ingrained in the structure of human society it remains visible and active in our own modern social order. The separation of Church and State, for instance, is only a vestigial insistence upon preserving what is left of the Dual System. On the other hand, present-day interpretations of Democracy go straight back to the time of Taurus, and are a continuance of the work of the Warrior Kings who took over the sole rulership of the Earth.

Other indications of the Dual System also remained. They are discussed elsewhere in this book. One may well ask, since Pisces – the Fishes – is the Age out of which we have just passed, why there was not a revival of the old Dual System under the 'double bodied' sign? One could reply with the question: Are we altogether sure there was not some such revival at some level of human operation?

During the time when the Dual Organisation was in effect, there are indications that the astrology of that time was also dual. Instead of the single circle of twelve consecutive signs in use now (and accepted as going back to the beginning of the Age of Taurus – the end of Gemini), there appears to have existed a *double zodiac*. Each circle consisted of six signs, and each sign occupied sixty degrees of the Heavenly circle. In other words, each sixty degrees segment of the Heavenly Round was occupied by two zodiacal signs, one of which belonged to the human or 'nocturnal' zodiac and the other to the solar or 'diurnal' zodiac.

. The nocturnal or lunar zodiac was the *exoteric* one, and applied to the Secular Kings and to their moiety. The diurnal or solar zodiac was *esoteric*, at least until the Age of Taurus (the Earth-Shaker), and pertained to the Divine Kings, the Children of the Sun and their moiety.

Horoscopes of people born in the Secular moiety would have been cast from the lunar zodiac, while those of people born into the Divine solar moiety would have been cast from the solar or diurnal wheel.

During the Age of Leo, the King-Priest existed in Atlantis, as representative of the Sky People, and the double zodiac was used, equating with the two types of people, Galactic and Non-Galactic.

About 9500 BC Poseid was submerged. In consequence, great east and west migrations of the people took place. Time moves on into the Sign of Cancer, the Crab (Babylonian: the Tortoise). The Book is hidden. Surviving Man is again taught how to build houses and eventually the Egyptian priests begin to work the single zodiac.

In the time of Gemini, the sign of the Twins, the six secondary signs were each given, in theory, thirty degrees out of the other six, and the twelve-sign one-track zodiac was formed. Astronomically, this is an unbalanced zodiac, since some signs do not occupy the full thirty degrees allotted to them, while other signs occupy more than thirty degrees.

The Age of Gemini represented the last stand of the Dual System before the coming of the Age of Taurus. During this New Age, the office of Priest-King was abolished, the single Warrior King took full charge, the cult of the Bull and the Earth Mother was established, the single zodiac adopted and the earth people took over entirely the management of their own affairs.

During the past ages comprising the more than 11,000 years since Poseid was said to have gone down to its oblivion, there may have been many mutations and many minglings among mankind. It may be that many of the different types of human-

ity that appeared in the world took on their identifying bodily
and cultural patterns within the period of upheaval and re-
gression that followed immediately upon the great catastrophe.
Isolated groups, although reduced to a nomadic existence,
would have wandered within definite geographical and natural
boundaries. Inbreeding and the necessities of survival in various environments would tend to emphasise certain physical
traits, and in so far as the genetic laws discovered by the
monk, Gregor Mendel, apply to human beings, distinctive
differences between peoples would become more pronounced,
resulting in what we now call, somewhat mistakenly, racial
characteristics.

Certainly, racial differences of this kind existed in Atlantean times. It would seem to be probable, however, that in
those days there was not the same variety and number of
recognisable patterns which now confuse the modern ethno-
grapher. The centuries of bad weather following the end of
Poseid's career must have had two general consequences.
Relatively small groups of human beings were isolated from
one another for a sufficient length of time to become characteristic 'breeds of men', and the terrible meteorological conditions made such a deep and lasting impression upon those
who survived that by the time we find them at the civilised
stage again, their foremost earthly divinities have become connected with the weather. There is even a very early story
among the Sumerians of a time when the sun was absent for
a long period and had to be coaxed back again.

O. R. Gurney quotes an ancient Hittite text.

Dust (?) – clouds beset the window, smoke (?) besets
the house, the embers on the hearth were choked (?), the
gods stifled (in the temple), the sheep stifled in the fold, the
oxen stifled in the stall, the ewe spurned her lamb, the cow
spurned her calf. . . . Barley and emmer wheat throve no
more, oxen, sheep and humans ceased to conceive and
those who were pregnant could not bear.[58]

At some time early in the third millennium BC the barriers
between these isolated and newly developed peoples began to
break down. Communication between them originated in the

form of conquest and has continued to be maintained in that form until the present day. International politics and possible military function remain strong determining factors in the location of roads and the design of aircraft. Our technological glory consists of a multitude of refinements overlaid upon basic principles of human nature as old as mankind, and still as operative.

All sorts of theories exist as to the reason for this beginning of history. Probably the most popular at the moment is that developing city civilisations grew great enough to impinge upon one another and conflict was inevitable. This is an opinion, however, based upon an assumption that two groups must always prove to be hostile to one another. History has many examples to hand which offer equal proof that this need not be true. It is only when one group believes that one of the two groups involved (either itself or the other) is either superior or inferior. Whichever way the combination works out there will be hostility, and this may descend to aggression, either as an uprising or as conquest. Self-esteem has brought about more bloodshed than any greed for goods or other loot.

Looking at history and legendary pre-history as a student of tradition must do, it becomes apparent that the kind of hostility which descends to murderous aggression arises between groups who have no actual basis for their assumption of superiority, either of their own or of the other fellow's.

When cultures of different patterns have an opportunity to come together, there is much that can be developed from an intelligent interchange between the two. Regrettably, in the course of recorded history, there has been little opportunity for such a level, and scope, of communication. Therefore, in age after age, and in case after case, we see the clash of two cultures, possibly equal or nearly so in value and development, but operating under different patterns and emphasising different essential human necessities, and inevitably, it is the conqueror who adopts something of the pattern (but not the spirit) of the conquered, and hands it down to his own conquerors in a diminished and distorted form.

Somewhere in the background of humanity there must be some strong and ineradicable reason for this idea of a superior group. Our friends among the evolutionists will say it is a development of personal vanity, that the chief of one tribe wishes to become the chief of two, and so on. They leave out of the argument, however, the noticeable fact that this is entirely untrue of the oldest, most 'primitive', so-called groups and tribes. These people, wherever they may be found in the world, are invariably peaceful monotheists with the greatest respect for one another, for their neighbours, and even for their women. The seed of conquest is not in them.

Mankind's multiplicity of little gods and his desire to make himself master of his neighbour is a comparatively late development in the world. Its origins are contemporaneous with his assertions that he is either in communication with people in or from the sky (and others of his fellows are not), or that he is descended from people in or from the sky (and others of his fellows are not).

Unless the whole human race is madder than we think it is, there must be some kind of background for these two extraordinary notions. The most obvious cause behind such apparently wild assertions would seem to be that at one time and up to a certain point in history, there was actually a group of men, or several groups of men, on Earth, who, for reasons unimaginable to humankind, undertook to guide, teach, and help to rule them, and that these people came, quite literally, *out of the sky*. We say, help to rule, because when mankind set up his imitation of the old system there were two co-reigning kings, the one representing the sky side, and the other representing the earth side. And such an unstable system could only have been made operative by a third and higher arbitrating authority, on any extensive scale.

The removal of that third and balancing factor had to come, eventually, for many important reasons, most of which we will consider on other pages.

Was the withdrawal of this balance the beginning of mankind's conquest of himself? There is traditional evidence that it may have been. Among the threads of this evidence there is the interesting fact that the seventh sign of the zodiac, Libra, the scales or balances, became an exoteric or publicly considered sign. The mystery of association with and communication with the people of the sky became the property of those among mankind who assumed the rulership of all. One human being dared to assume both the office of priest and that of king.

We find the struggle still going on in our own day, with arguments being put forth concerning the secular rights of pontiffs, and the political privileges of prelates.

The races which formed themselves after the destruction of Poseid have long since met and intermingled. Some have survived, here and there, one of the oldest of these being the Celts. Most of them, however, have blended together and given rise to still more modern elements, groups of humanity that can be looked upon as definite stocks. Out of the melting-pot we live in today, three great general groups appear to be emerging. Will the glory and the culmination of the next great cycle of 25,000 years into which we have entered, go to only one of them, or to all three, or to some unimaginable – and, possibly to our kind of man, distasteful – combination of them all?

If the voice of history carries any weight at all, it will probably be the last possibility which will come to pass.

8. Man into God: Osiris

From time to time we require certain things from distant *entrepots,* and it is our habit to obtain them in due course . . . – *Chang*

The nature of Osiris appears to be more like that of a man than like that of a god. He has character, and a personality, and his story, like that of Jesus in our own time, maintained a hold upon the emotions of the Egyptians for 3,000 years.

R. T. Rundle Clark writes: 'Osiris is the most vivid achievement of the Egyptian imagination. He is also the most complex. Although not the Lord of the Universe, he is not therefore a subordinate deity. The High God, creator and determiner of fate, is a theological concept, the supreme personification of power, will and wisdom, eternal and ineffable – to some extent beyond the power of the imagination to understand, to be apprehended in symbolic terms. Osiris is quite different, he demands sympathy. He is the completely helpless one, the essential victim. Yet he is avenged and his passion has an end at last, when justice and order are re-established on Earth. The other gods are transcendent, distinct from their worshippers. Osiris, however, is immanent. He is the sufferer with all mortality but at the same time he is all the power of revival and fertility in the world. He is the power of growth in plants and of reproduction in animals and human beings. He is both dead and the source of all living. Hence to become Osiris is to become one with the cosmic cycles of death and rebirth.'[54]

It would appear then that Osiris has all the characteristics we would expect to find in a real man who had once lived, reigned, and taught in the world, and who had subsequently been defied by the people who later made a religion out of his teachings and his life story. This would seem to be much more than a 'vivid achievement of the Egyptian imagination', unless we are willing to suppose that the Egyptians were a whole lot less practical and down to earth than their other achievements would make them out to be.

If we look at Osiris and see him as a real man, one who lived, suffered and died like other men, and who taught his people the art of civilised living, then the rest of his story comes out of the mists of mythology and takes more reasonable shape. It can be read as ancient history embalmed in myth and mummified in religion, but history, none the less, and capable of translation in terms of human activity.

Rundle Clark states: 'There is no definite evidence as yet that Osiris was worshipped in the prehistoric period. Even if he were, that would not imply that the primitive figure had much in common with the highly developed god we encounter in historical times. A symbol of Osiris has recently been found that dates from the beginning of historical times, about 3000 BC, otherwise there is no specific proof of his existence until he appears in the Pyramid Texts which were inscribed between 2400 and 2200 BC. In these texts he is already fully developed, not only already provided with a complete mythology but a carefully thought out theology as well. Moreover, the power and pretensions of the god increase as time goes on. Many have supposed that Osiris was the god of the common people as opposed to the more aristocratic Re, the Sun God of the Pharaohs. This may be partially true, for there are no signs of religious controversy between the devotees of the two gods. Theologians tried on several occasions to reconcile their claims but without complete success. During the New Kingdom Amun – the successor of Re as the official High God – acquired an almost monotheistic character, rendering other gods unnecessary. This, however, failed to have lasting effect. During the last millennium BC the popularity of Osiris grew steadily until, under the Ptolemies who ruled Egypt from 323 BC to the Roman conquest, he became Serapis, the Lord of the universe in all its aspects.'[55]

Looking at all this, it begins to show evidence of that sort of 'promotion up the line' by which human beings have consistently deified certain of their heroes. The very fact that there is 'no definite evidence as yet that Osiris was worshipped in the prehistoric period' bears this out. Before 3000 BC it is likely that the people knew more about him, and while he may have been venerated as the heroic founder of their 'order' or way of life, he would have been, for them, still an historical figure. It is only in 3000 BC that the first symbol of Osiris appears. By that time he was beginning to lose some of his historical reality and had taken the first step towards his deification. It is only when concrete reality begins to fade that Man resorts to symbols and begins to project interpretations, and later on, to universalise his concepts. Conversely, when Man wishes to invest someone or something with an aura of mystic potency, he creates a symbol, around which he can hang his more abstract ideas.

Certainly, 600 to 800 years after the appearance of this first known symbol of Osiris, there is worship, theology and mythology. 'Moreover, the power and pretensions of the god increase as time goes on.' The process of deification is complete by that time.

The highly individual and personal character of Osiris survived, however, even the near-monotheism of Amun, and 'the popularity of Osiris grew steadily until . . . he became Serapis, the Lord of the universe in all its aspects'.

The first aspect of Osiris, his genealogical connections, is probably an interpolation of the priests. It is theological, and belongs to that later period in the history of the veneration of Osiris, when it was necessary to explain his relationship with the heavenly hierarchy. Because of this it will be seen to have a wider interpretation as well as a broader and more general meaning than the merely personal or individual. In fact, it is the old story of the two kinds of Man again, the Elder and the Younger Brother, born of the Earth (Geb) and the Sky (Nut).

Rundle Clark wrote: 'Osiris was a king who ruled over Egypt and who taught the arts of civilisation to his subjects. It is Osiris who is in communication with "the stars" as the New Kingdom hymn says.

"He established justice throughout both banks (of the Nile), he put the son in his father's place . . .
overthrowing the adversary with might and power . . .
(Earth) saw how excellent he was and entrusted the kingship to him to lead the Two Lands into prosperity."

'In typical Oriental hyperbole the encomium ends with:

"His crown clove the sky and consorted with the stars." '56

Six hundred years after his first appearance we find him fitted out with a complete theology and mythology. One might suppose that if it were possible to continue on back in time toward the source of his history, one would find more and more truth and less mystery. How far is it permissible to go? Let us look back at the available data as the Egyptians have passed it along to us.

Osiris taught the art of Agriculture to the Egyptians. Let us look at that from a point of view other than the Egyptian, for a moment, and say Osiris is the name the Egyptians passed along for the individual who originally taught them how to control the Nile waters, irrigate their fields, and grow their own food, instead of gathering it as the animals do.

Archaeology provides us with further data. Farming, the weaving of linen textiles, and the making of baskets are already well developed by 4500 BC. This means they were really taught, and learned – and, indeed, perfected – to a high level of technical skill some time *within the same 1,500 year period* during which earth man learned to build rectangular houses, plaster floors and walls, and make thumb-pressed bricks.

This makes it possible to put Osiris down, then, as either one of the Men from the other world who arrived to teach mankind, or one of their earthly associates. It was only far later, when the knowledge of that other world as a real, three-dimensional 'island in the sky' had faded away, that people began to assume that anybody who came from the sky must be from some so-called spiritual or immaterial other world. This idea would gain credence if some remnant of tradition also stated that an Osiris could assume or discard the chemical bodily appearance as well. When the real explanations go, mysticism and theological interpretation take over. Everything then begins to mean something else, and the original individual is inflated by all this dogmatic and hierarchical wind to fill the Universe. Then men appear to have a new god, suddenly. Actually, however, they have only a new name for the old, original one, Most High Creator, in whom mankind first believed before these expanded and expanding younger inventions arose to 'displace their elder brother'.

But to return to our timing. If we can safely say that Osiris was one of the teachers in the world who actually did arrive from another one and instruct people in such arts and crafts as Agriculture and Architecture, it will certainly not be stretching things very much to infer that in this case, Osiris was one of the first Masonic Brethren who went about in the world 'making masons'. There is much material in the symbolism and worship of Osiris, which, when compared with modern or even revised Masonic lore and usage, makes such a conclusion all but inevitable.

By a perfectly natural process of association, interpretation, and embroidery, he was elevated, stage by stage, down through the centuries, from hero to universal God. Myths were made to explain interpretations, and in course of examination new ideas cropped up which, in their turn, had to be explained. Finally, we arrive at the tangled web through which the present-day investigator must peer and probe if he is to find his way back to that first simple encounter between members of two brother races.

Referring back now to our Egyptian time-table of chronology, Rundle Clark says: 'Osiris' claims were disputed by Seth. Osiris taught mankind the arts of civilisation. Another (and alternative) Golden Age.'[57]

In the Bible and in all such old narratives of what happened long ago, names of individuals represent whole groups. Seth was such a group, and Osiris here becomes a line or hierarchy (or dynasty) of Osirises. As in all the twin-stories, the younger and more earthly brother wishes to depose his reigning elder brother, to usurp his position, and to take power and control into his own hands. This is always disastrous, if attempted prematurely, but it is what usually happens. It will continue to happen until the younger brother learns his lessons and settles down to making a good job of governing himself. The thirst for power and self-aggrandisement are his two most terrible snares.

The story of the shutting up of Osiris in a chest which is then thrown into the water and which floats away sounds profoundly like the old story of that part of the race of Man who went away from the Earth, through the waters of Space, to live somewhere else. This is reinforced by the further item of information that the chest or box was lodged in a tree in another country, and that it remained there long enough for the tree to grow around it. Have we here an allusion to the Polar Tree, to the Sky, connecting the water symbol with the ocean of Space?

Osiris does not come back from the other world to reign again on Earth. The story, as it has come down to us, tells us that it is his 'son', conceived and brought up by the priestess-wife of Osiris, who, when he comes to his maturity, establishes again a measure of Osirian order.

After Seth and his confederates had done away with Osiris, there followed a period of 'confusion and terror', in sharp contrast to the orderly state of affairs associated with the golden age of the reign of Osiris.

It is the female side that attempts to rediscover Osiris and all that he means to the world, and to restore him to life, i.e. to bring back the knowledge of civilisation and its ways that was lost through the nefarious actions of Seth. Even the wife of Seth helps in all this! That is to say, even the women belonging to the earth-human side agree with and join with those descended from the sky-side in the preservation and restoration of the Osirian traditions.

Do we have here an echo of the conflict between the old, primeval veneration of the Great Mother by her priestesses, and the establishment of the masculine deity of the usurping warrior earth-man?

Isis, which is to say, the priestesses of the dead and departed Osiris, of whom the wife of Seth, Nephthys is one, manage to recover the parts of the body of Osiris, the knowledge and traditions. They bind them together again, but they cannot really revive them completely and make Osiris live again cn Earth. They can, however, bring them back to life sufficiently to instruct at least one man, or group of men, willing to listen. And so it is that Osiris was revived just enough to allow Isis to conceive his son. Horus was the son of the murdered king in the sense that he had been given the knowledge Osiris had brought into the world – the symbolic life of Osiris – in so far as the priestess of the Delta had been able to preserve it.

Before the birth of Horus and all through the period of his growing up, Isis is said to have hidden him and herself in the Nile Delta. When Horus was grown, he mustered the followers of Osiris and attacked Seth, the usurper. In time the men who had been instructed in the Osirian traditions felt strong enough to try to overthrow the supplanter and to re-establish the old Osirian way of life. This led to a long and bitter civil war. Into the middle of this conflict, suddenly we are told that one of the gods (was it a sky person?) steps in and tries to arbitrate. This personage is called Hermes by the Greek writer, and Hermes is the Greek name for Thoth. He was successful in getting the participants to take their quarrel before the Celestial counterpart of the modern-day United Nations, that is, the Council of the Gods. However, apparently Horus had to resort to battle again and eventually succeeded in defeating both Seth and his followers.

After this, we are told, there was communication between Horus and Osiris, and the reign of Horus was the beginning of the earthly monarchy.

I believe we have here the whole story, in outline, of the re-civilisation of mankind on earth, and of the establishment of the line of priest-kings that lasted until, strangely enough, Menes took both crowns for himself and united Upper and Lower Egypt, perhaps as early as 3200 BC.

Osiris belongs to the Age of Gemini, the Twins, before the departure of the Sky People. He is a sky king. His overthrow by Seth represents the time when affairs were turned over to the men of earth to try and run things in their own way. From the content of this story, the turning over of authority was not all that peaceful, in the case of the Egyptians, and may have been premature. Earth man asserted himself against those he deemed his 'overlords', translating their motives in terms of his own. The result was 'confusion and terror', to quote the old records, and a deterioration of the social structure.

Finally, however, the priest-kings who had been instructed in the ancient traditions of the sky-side, as collected and preserved by the priestesses, were able to put the usurper in his place and restore a measure of what Man had enjoyed during the Golden Age of the Divine Kings. Horus, the post-humous son of Osiris, represents the earthly dynasties, established in the Age of Taurus, after 4699 BC, and which lasted until about the year 3200 BC – the time of the founding of the first dynasty of the united kingdom under Menes, and the approximate date of the first known symbol of Osiris.

If we look back a bit, we find that we have quoted Rundle Clark, as saying: 'A symbol of Osiris has recently been found that dates from the beginning of historical times, about 3000 BC.' It is passing strange that this symbol, which infers the beginning of worship, should coincide with the taking over, by an earth man, of both sides of the system to which Osiris belonged, in his time, as a Teacher from elsewhere. Within about 2,000 years he had become god-like, if not a god.

This is all too reminiscent of what happened to another messenger who was born in Bethlehem about 3,000 years later, and who, like Osiris, was perfidiously slain, but who also had, surpassing his more ancient example, the power of bodily resurrection.

It is not enough to say that early Man (as we call him) made up stories to explain to himself the mysteries of seed and sun, and the cycle of the year. He lived in a much more primitive way than modern Man, without all those conveniences and the ease of ready communication that have given men of a later era the leisure time so necessary to the pursuit of imagination and fancy. On the whole, early Man was probably far less imaginative than we are.

Thousands of years ago a strange and significant journey was made. Even today, the act of travelling from Egypt to England and back, would be considered by most people as an outstanding event in their lives, leaving aside the fact that modern air transport has brought the flying time between London and Cairo to a matter of only a few hours.

Imagine, though, a journey between Egypt and England seven or eight millennia ago, when there were no jet airliners, and only the most primitive methods of travel were available. Madame Blavatsky records such an event:

'. . . there are records which show Egyptian priests – Initiates

– journeying in a north-westerly direction by *land*, via what became later the Straits of Gibraltar: turning North and travelling through the future Phoenician settlements of Southern Gaul: then still farther North, until reaching Carnac (Morbihan) they turned to the West again and arrived, *still travelling by land*, on the north-western promontory of the New Continent. (Or on what are now the British Isles, which were not yet detached from the main continent in those days.) "The ancient inhabitants of Picardy could pass into Great Britain without crossing the Channel. The British Isles were united to Gaul by an isthmus which has since disappeared." '58

What was the object of their long journey? And how far back must we place the date of such visits? . . . The fact of their crossing from France to Great Britain by land may give an idea of the date when such a journey could have been performed on terra firma.

'It was when:

"The level of the Baltic and of the North Sea was 400 feet higher than it is at the present day. The valley of the Somme was not hollowed to the depth it has now attained: Sicily was joined to Africa, Barbary to Spain. Carthage, the Pyramids of Egypt, the palaces of Uxmal and Palenque, were not yet in existence, and the bold navigators of Tyre and Sidon, who at a later date were to undertake their perilous voyages along the coasts of Africa were yet unborn." '59

Madame Blavatsky, of course, then proceeds to give some fantastic figures for the dates involved. But we must remember that elsewhere in her writings she states, with emphasis, that true dates and real figures are 'secrets of Initiation' and are not to be disclosed, at least at that writing.

What then has the more advanced and detailed information available in our own day to say about this supposed connection between the British Isles and the continental mainland? First of all, research confirms the existence of the landbridge. Second, it can give an approximate date, up until which time the travelling Initiates might have walked all that way dry-shod as they are said to have done. By geological and archaeological evidence, they could not have made their journey in that manner very much later than 6000 BC.

What were they looking for? Was it a missionary journey? Somehow this seems doubtful. These priests were said to have been initiates, and in antiquity this was a term associated less with what we could call religion and more with what we now know as learning and science. Did their traditions tell them of a source of knowledge in that far-off West Country?

We feel it is only logical, and certainly substantiated by such traditions as still survive in our own time, that they did. Being true Initiates, and real Priests, according to their own meanings of those words, they made a great Pilgrimage, seeking what was, for them, already an ancient Holy Place. 'On the north-western promontory of the New Continent' (Europe – which was new in the sense that their forebears had only recently in the course of their history, come there to live after the final destruction of Poseid). Later, this promontory was to become the south-western part of England.

We do not believe those elder wise-men would have travelled so far under what must have been very primitive conditions, only to erect such impossibly huge and impossibly exact astronomical effigies as those in the Somerset Zodiac. However, they would, in all likelihood, have undertaken such an extended Odyssey in the hope of being able to rediscover such an historical and scientific treasure, and to have an opportunity to study it.

And this is what some of us believe happened.

If they arrived in sufficient numbers, and if they could have enlisted sufficient co-operation from the local inhabitants, they might have left some additions of their own. On the other hand, if they considered any tampering to be in the nature of a profanation, then they would not have done such a thing. It would depend entirely upon their own peculiar bias, whether they were more scientific than priestly, or the other way round. If their thinking lay on the scientific side, then perhaps they would have left their signatures in the form of some addition of their own to the already existing effigies. If they thought more in terms of religion and the sanctity of the site, then almost certainly they would not.

Was the priest-initiate who later became that ruler of Egypt, and taught the Egyptians, both the arts of Civilisation and Agriculture, among this pilgrim band? By the time of Menes,

3000 years later, one such had become a god-figure, yet it is almost certain he was a real man, and a king of the ninth Egyptian Nome.

Did the first Osiris bring at least a part of his wisdom back with him from the ancient Temple of the Stars in Somerset? It would seem to be well within the realms of possibility that he did.

1. The author seated in one of the giant stones at Avebury

2. Silbury Hill, Avebury

3. A reconstruction of Avebury as it may have appeared in pre-historic times

4. The Uffington White Horse and the neighbouring hill-fort, Uffington Castle

5. A pre-historic cemetery, a mile and a half south-west of
   Stonehenge, including a long barrow, as well as bowl, bell
   and disc barrows, showing similarity to cigar and disc-
   shaped flying objects

6. Stonehenge

7. Four of the 10,000 menhirs at Carnac, Brittany

8. The Pyramids at Giza, near Cairo

9. Statue of the Sphinx at Giza, near Cairo

10. 'A silent and immovable stone', lying in a quarry at Baalbeck

11. The Gate of the Sun at Tiahuanaco, Bolivia
Above, front view; *below*, rear view

9. The Corner Stone

We may expect no mercy, but we may hope for neglect . . . we have a heritage to cherish and bequeath. – The High Lama

Is it not feasible that the knowledge Osiris and his companions brought back from Britain, given them by those who were in a position to impart it at the most respected and sacred place on earth – the Temple of the Stars in Somerset – formed at least a part of the groundwork upon which the Great Pyramid came to be built some millennia later? The Golden Age of the Osirises lasted about 2,000 years, from around 6000 BC to 4000 BC. The Sky People by that time were beginning to withdraw from the active affairs of mankind, but before they finally departed, they left, as we believe, a permanent legacy for the men of the future.

The Great Pyramid at Giza has long been credited by archaeological authorities to Cheops (the Greeks couldn't pronounce his real name, Khufu, and called him Cheops) who was supposed to have built it about 2700 BC.

According to I. E. S. Edwards, there were altogether about eighty pyramids in Egypt, some of which he tells us are now reduced 'to little more than sand and rubble, but they are still recognisable to the archaeologists as having once been pyramids'.[60]

Egyptologists say the first pyramid was that built by Zoser in the Third Dynasty, in 2686 BC. This was a Step Pyramid at Saqqara. Then followed another of the same type, built by Sekhemkhet, also in the Third Dynasty, at the same location. Next came Layer Pyramids at Zawiyet al-Aryan and Meidum. Then, at Dahshur, Seneferu in the Fourth Dynasty, constructed what is termed a Bent Pyramid. After that, the experts say, Cheops, in the Fourth Dynasty, erected the Great Pyramid at Giza. Subsequently, Djedefre built one at Abu Roash and two others, those of Chephren and Mycerinus, were also erected at Giza, close to the Great Pyramid.

113

The Great Pyramid contains in its dimensions astronomical information which is becoming available only in the latter half of the twentieth century, AD. The mathematical calculations which go into this sort of knowledge require, nowadays, the services of calculating machines which take up thousands of feet of floor space and involve a technology of which the Ancient Egyptians themselves could have known nothing. Thousands of years were to pass before Benjamin Franklin flew the kite that demonstrated the nature of lightning and suggested how it might be tamed. Almost 200 years later, Nikola Tesla gave the world more developments in this one fundamental field of discovery than this present-day civilisation has been able to accept. However, something similar may have happened at the time those ambitious pilgrims from Egypt (including, perhaps, the man who was to become the first great instructor – and king – in the Faiyum) made their long journey to the most western promontory of the New Continent.

Davidson and Aldersmith, in their book about the Pyramid, worked out several systems of chronology that were built into the architecture of the Great Pyramid. One, for instance, is zodiacal. Another is astronomical. The zodiacal system, or Epoch, commences with the Age of Taurus, at 4699 BC. Still another scale begins at the Autumnal Equinox of 4000 BC.

One of the Great Pyramid's most interesting astronomical alignments, however, has to do with the position and slope of the descending passage (from the entrance of the pyramid down to the pit). On two dates, 8144 BC and 3434 BC, the then Pole Star, Alpha Draconis, would be observable in a certain way.

'. . . at the time of both dates – but not at any date preceding the latter, succeeding the former, or intervening between the two dates – the pole-star of ancient times, Alpha Draconis, would be seen by an observer at the bottom of the Pyramid's descending passage precisely at midnight of the Autumnal Equinox. Strictly speaking, the condition would hold approximately for several years before and after both dates. (The accurate conditions of observation for the precise alignment require the observer to sight the star through two apertured diaphragms or partitions fixed into the passage at a considerable interval apart.)'[61]

The latter date is far too late in time for the building of the Pyramid, even had this been accomplished by Cheops. If the precise alignment of the descending passage upon the old Pole Star is accidental, then this fantastic coincidence must be added to the already overlong chain of fortuitous correspondences of mathematical and astronomical data relating to the Pyramid, the combined weight of which must, figuratively, outweigh the enormous structure itself.

Such accuracy could hardly have been achieved without direct observation. Therefore, it would appear to be reasonable to believe that the true date for the construction of the Great Pyramid corresponds to the earlier date of this alignment of the descending passage with the then Pole Star.

Apparently, the alignment was checked at the later of the two dates, for there are, inside the descending passage on both walls, scored lines which mark the date, 2144 BC. Davidson and Aldersmith take this to indicate that the date of the Pyramid's foundation was 2144 BC, but this date is after the biblical date of the flood associated with the Semitic Noah by a couple of hundred years. For a variety of reasons we prefer the earlier date. Doubtless, in 2144 BC, the priests would want to check the alignment as part of their astronomical observations. At that time, be it remembered, the inscriptions upon the outer casing stones were still there to be read. Did they include instructions relating to occurrences of this nature?

Nearly all these outer casing stones have now disappeared. They have been taken away by looters down the centuries, and many went into the building of the town of Giza. However, we have the testimony of Herodotus who saw the inscriptions himself, and who said that they were on polished stones. Other travellers stated that the inscriptions would, altogether, cover more than 10,000 words of writing. William of Boldensole, a German knight, reported in the fourteenth century that he had seen them written in various languages.

And what more did they have to say to mankind 'in a number of languages'? We will never know. Mankind's depredations have erased for ever the key to this great mystery, which can now be unlocked only with difficulty and patient calculation.

A point to note in connection with the earlier date, 3434 BC, is this: up to that time there had been a degree of civilisation established in the world, particularly in Egypt and in what was to become Sumer, so far as can be determined from archaeological evidence. It was a village civilisation based upon primitive agriculture, together with home industries such as weaving and the making of pottery by hand. The basis of social organisation was probably the matriarchal clan, which was a way of life that had been handed down from the Stone Age. It was ancient, traditional and conservative, and it produced the sedentary cultures that held mankind together and gave him roots, once he had been taught to build permanent houses and the women had learned how to cultivate the ground and produce plants for food and for the manufacture of the textiles that replaced the Stone Age 'coats of skins'.

All this had been accomplished under the tutelage of the gods, the Men from the Sky. Now it was time for mankind to take his destiny into his own hands and to see what he could make of it. In no other way could he ever develop his latent and accidentally suppressed potentialities. There was more, much more, ahead of mankind, than the life of a simple nursling of his so-called gods.

Two modes of life had been offered him: the settled agricultural system, and the still mobile but well-organised pastoral existence. The time had come for the two to meet and merge, and the blending was something mankind must work out for himself. For obvious reasons it could not be enforced without enfeebling the result. Cain and Abel must come to terms, and as the biblical story figuratively tells us, the inevitable clash involved a certain amount of murder. In the end, however, and even though the murder still goes on, there has come into the world a realisation that brothers at least ought to be one another's keepers.

By 3000 BC the divine dynasties in Egypt and among the Sumerians had become historical, if not legendary. The golden age when the god-kings walked with mankind and taught him the ways of civilisation lay far enough in the past to form the traditional stories which served, in those days, in the place of history. The Sky People had gone home, and mankind was learning to solve his problems by himself. He began with conquest. The sedentary people in the villages and little city states began to move in upon one another. Menes united Upper and Lower Egypt. The mobile people, no longer restrained by the presence of their tutors, moved away from their normal ranges and came down upon the sedentary cultures, and the ferment that was to produce a world got under way.

Alone, or so we think, at the apex of the Nile delta, there stood the Grand Memorial, 'an altar to the Lord in the midst of the Land of Egypt, and a pillar at the border thereof to the Lord',[62] the great corner-stone of the new Taurean Age, the Great Pyramid – gift of the people from the sky.

For a time child-mankind must have respected it, but after a while, and after the manner of children in all ages, he forgot what it was supposed to mean to him, grew careless of it, and partially destroyed it. What happened to the gilded capstone? No one knows. The beautiful white casing stones were ripped off to build the town of Giza and heaven only knows what else. Earlier, when it was still a sacred object, kings tried to copy it for their tombs, in order to satisfy their vanity. Nowadays, it stands neglected and misunderstood, while another adolescent civilisation reaches for the stars and does not understand the source of the urge that sends it into Space.

And so we therefore submit that the Great Pyramid was erected by the Sky People themselves as a parting present about 3434 BC. This was to serve as a reminder of earth man's past Atlantean heritage and also as a repository of knowledge for the future.

There is a later legend among the Arabs concerning the building of this great structure. An unknown king, called Surid, is said, according to the story, to have built the pyramid at Giza as the result of a dream he had foretelling a flood. He is supposed to have constructed the pyramid, not primarily as a tomb, but as a place of refuge for people in the event of catastrophe. Furthermore, the legend tells that Surid inscribed the prophecies given in his dream on the polished outer casing stones of the Great Pyramid. Who was Surid? He is not known to orthodox Egyptologists. Nevertheless, the legend of this king has survived.

If Cheops built the Great Pyramid, it was the biggest mathematical accident that ever happened. It has been reported that Cheops' name has been found on a block in the Chambers of Construction above the King's Chamber in the Pyramid. However, it is also known that long after the Pyramid was built, someone forced a tunnel through to the Chambers of Construction. What for, and why? Nobody knows.

I would like to bring in here the example of another, later Egyptian Pharaoh – Ramesses II. Werner Keller, in *The Bible as History*, writes: 'Ramesses II, the "Great", has given archaeologists many a hard nut to crack. Apparently his vanity was even greater than his passion for building. He never hesitated to deck himself in borrowed plumes: posterity would marvel at the great builder Rameses II! And indeed it did. The experts could hardly grasp at first how it came about that on so many temples, public buildings and in other places they came upon the cipher "Ramesses II". But when they examined the buildings a little more closely the explanation was plain. Many of these buildings must have been built centuries before Ramesses II. To pander to his own vanity, however, Ramesses II decided to have his monogram carved on them all.'[63]

We postulate, then, that the Great Pyramid credited to Cheops was, in reality, constructed around 3434 BC. After a lapse of time amounting to some 600 years, the Egyptians made their first effort to emulate this superb monument, and their work resulted in Zoser's Step Pyramid. I have no quarrel with the dates given by archaeology for the construction of the other pyramids, but I maintain that they are all attempts to copy the Great Pyramid. Eventually the pyramids of Chephren and Mycerinus were erected on the same plateau at Giza as the Great Pyramid. They cover an area at their bases respectively of 708 feet square and 356 feet square. Although they are marvellous buildings, they do not attain the standard of the incomparable Great Pyramid.

The workmanship and accuracy that went into the construction of the Great Pyramid is literally 'out of this world'. No building contractor anywhere in the world today could achieve such perfection. Leonard Cottrell quotes Sir Flinders Petrie:

'. . . the mean thickness of the eastern joint of the northern casing stones is 0.020 inch (one fiftieth of an inch), therefore the mean variation of the cutting of the stone from a straight line is but 0.01 inch (one hundredth part of an inch) of seventy-five inches up the face . . . these joints, with an area of thirty-five square feet each, were not only worked as finely as this, but cemented throughout. Though the stones were brought as close as one five-hundredth of an inch, or, in fact, into contact, and the main opening of the joint was one fiftieth of an inch, yet the builders managed to fill the joint with cement, despite the great area of it, and the weight of the stone, some sixteen tons. . . .'[64]

Everything about the whole Pyramid staggers the imagination. It is, in truth, a creation of the gods.

It will be recalled that Peck pointed out that the origin of the zodiac probably goes back to a time very close to 13000 BC. He also added it must have been conceived in some fairly cloudless country near the latitude of twenty-five degrees north of the Equator. He suggested Egypt, but he was an astronomer of good repute and remained well within the limits of scientific acceptance. He said nothing about Atlantis, which immediately springs to mind as a more probable place of origin for the zodiac in that time.

Tradition tells us Egypt was a colony of Atlantis.

The Great Pyramid has been thought by many to be a part of our Atlantean heritage. Then why not the Sphinx as well? Is the Sphinx a symbolic monument to both Atlantis and to her science of the stars? Does the Sphinx in her combined forms of woman and lion recall, and still reveal to those who have eyes to see, the original construction of the zodiac as we know it now, in Atlantis, under the sign of Virgo, 15,000-odd years ago when Virgo occupied the position of First Sign? Was wisdom 'born', indeed, from a virgin, and particularly from the Heavenly Virgin herself, because when men first mapped the dependable stars, did they take the symbol of a young maid for the first division of their zodiac because it was the first? For if we go backward 15,000 years, give or take a few, and if we play fair with the Egyptians by using their figure for the length of a zodiacal great age and for the length of one twelfth of such an age, or, one sign, we find that the stars that rose with the Vernal Equinox were the stars of Virgo!

Then why not a statue of a maid, and be done with it? Why add the body of a lion? Here, if we are dealing with the astrological eras, we come to a very clear and beautiful symbolic statement of the decline, downfall and catastrophic end of Atlantis, stated boldly and imaginatively in straightforward astrological terms for all to see.

This Sphinx, this monument in symbol to the astrologers of Ancient Atlantis, tells us that what began with the Virgin ended with the Lion. The head and breast are those of a woman, but the body is that of the Lion, the sign of Leo. And that body is recumbent, in the case of the great Sphinx. Some sort of decline or going down is associated with the Lion symbol here.

If we look again at available dates, and if we continue to play fair according to the Egyptian rules, using the Egyptian numbers, what do we find? We discover an astonishing and revealing thing: that the most agreed upon date for the submergence of the last remaining island of Atlantis, Poseid (or Poseidonis), is given as 9564 BC – and we find that date coming well toward the end of the Age of Leo, the time of the Lion.

In the *Tarot*, the tenth Major Trump is called the Wheel. On it is depicted a great wheel with figures around its rim. One of these figures is a sphinx. Does this Wheel, among other things, represent the great, nearly 26,000-year long cycle of the precession of the equinoxes? And, is the presence of the sphinx upon it stating some astrological and historical facts we have been thinking of in connection with this enigmatical monument? Surely, anyone who accepts or even entertains the idea that the *Tarot* has come down to us from Atlantean times might well be excused for harbouring such a notion.

The Sphinx is, also, surely representative of the two races of mankind, the heavenly and the earthly counterparts, and, at the same time, of humanity today, a mixture of both sides of the street – heavenly man as he was originally created and animal-man.

Due to certain habits of thought, of which the strictly disciplinary methods of teaching are only one example, we are accustomed to thinking about the Great Pyramid in connection with Egypt alone. Similarly, we are accustomed to thinking about any other monument in terms of its immediate geographical surroundings. This is because we have been taught to believe that mankind before the age of Columbus and the Elizabethan seamen, could get no farther away from home than he could paddle a dugout canoe, or sail with great difficulty in some small craft we would not be willing to risk our own lives in on a small lake in calm weather.

Actually, the extent of communication and trade in ancient times all over the world is amazing. Here again, we must be willing to face facts, however much they may disagree with modern historical acceptances and theory. Colonel Braghine shows how Plutarch's 'Meropa's Kingdom' mentioned in his treatise *On Lunar Spots* must have been South American, through tracing the origin of the word back to the Quichua language. Then, among many other instances, he goes on to tell of an incident recorded by Pomponius Mela in the *Chronographia* citing the reference (iii, 5, viii) 'which is the oldest preserved geographical treatise, and Pliny (Hist. Natur. ii, 67) both tell us, that in 62 BC, a boat, full of red-skinned people of an unknown origin, was thrown up by the sea-waves on the German coast'.[65] If, even at this late date, people managed to cross the Atlantic Ocean from Labrador to Germany (as it was concluded by 1553, as Braghine points out, these castaways had done), then certainly when Atlantis was at its height, and presumably even Poseid was on the point of going down, such trips must have been routine.

If we are to get any sort of realistic picture of the interrelation of cultures and their remains in ancient times, we will find it necessary to expand our horizons toward those experienced by practical, down to earth sailor-men and travellers, who lived and moved about the world in any given era.

Knowing this, then, it becomes certain that we cannot think about the Great Pyramid, the Somerset Zodiac, Stonehenge and Poseid, as separate and unrelated phenomena.

From the very fact of the possibility of communication between these areas, and from the known predilection of humanity to get up and go wherever it can, by whatever means happens to be available, we must assume at least the possibility of a connection. We need not attempt to prove this connection as an incontrovertible fact. Proof proves itself upon sufficient accumulation of data.

Therefore, it should be within the bounds of propriety for us to examine apparently far-flung and unrelated items like the Great Pyramid and the Zodiac in Somerset, in the light of any and all data we can uncover. The range of our new horizon will be all that territory through which the men of that time wandered and in which they left traces of themselves. In the process of this study we should be allowed access to any and all information it is possible to obtain, without regard to its official accepted classification. An age of scientific progress ought to be an age of revelation. No valid information should be withheld or restricted ('classified') simply because it lies outside a particular field or discipline. Let us dare to synthesise then, and see what we can uncover. We may not prove anything, for proof, after all, is an individual matter. We are only looking and pretend to do no more, but we are looking in a different light – a light that penetrates through a little more time and into a little more space. By that light, perhaps we can give mankind his due for being a bit more and for doing a bit more than has been officially credited to him by Authority.

Let us begin by considering Egypt, the British Isles, and Poseid, not as widely separated and non-communicating areas, but as the parts of one whole the ancient writers assumed them to be – sections of the vanished Atlantean Empire. References, books even, abound to state and to support this thesis. We need not go into detail here, then, upon that point. So let us switch on our strange light and get on with our looking. The name of the light is quite familiar to everybody. It is called Geography.

The area illuminated is a triangle, the corners of which lie in the Atlantic Ocean, in Egypt, and which takes in at its apex the British Isles. Actually, we shall be dealing with two triangles, one the image of the other, but first let us go to the

Landmark of our Fathers with which we are all familiar, the Great Pyramid itself, and do a little measuring. And we will talk about something called triangulation, but only briefly and for the sake of clarity.

The Oxford Dictionary says: 'triangulate, v.t. Make triangular; divide (area, etc.) into triangle for surveying purposes; determine (height, distance, etc.) thus.'

The Great Pyramid at Giza has for long been thought of as some sort of corner-stone of wisdom well and truly laid in this earth. We propose to follow this tradition and to take it quite literally for the corner-stone of our geographical triangulation, and supposing it to be a good corner-stone we will presume to extract from it an item of pertinent information. This datum is the angle, or slope of the triangle we are about to discover. And all this while we will remember that it was the Egyptians who used the three stakes and knotted cord of three, four, and five units to redetermine and to square up the corners of their fields after each annual inundation, even though in this instance we are dealing not with a square but with the profile of a pyramid.

Davidson and Aldersmith give the angle of the slope of the Great Pyramid as a precise 51 degrees 51 minutes 14.3 seconds.[66] On a small globe and using even the best transparent protractor available it is, of course, impossible to erect a triangle to such a degree of accuracy. It is comparatively easy, however, to translate the measurement into the nearest whole number, 52. For all practical purposes that will be near enough. The margin of error will be negligible.

If we take, then, as our base-line the parallel of latitude at the site of the Great Pyramid, and run a line north-westward at a slope of 52 degrees, that line will touch the northernmost tip of Scotland at a point nearly due north of the city of Madrid in Spain.

If we take this point as the northern or upper point of the triangle, the apex of our geographical pyramid, and proceed to construct the other side, where do we find the other base corner? At a point in the Atlantic Ocean, on the mid-Atlantic ridge, that rather more than roughly corresponds to the most usually agreed upon location of Poseid, that last remnant of the old Atlantean continent.

Of course, this could be all sheer coincidence. However, if we take the pyramid we have constructed and move it bodily southward until its base-line touches the tropic of Cancer, that dotted line on the globe marking the point of the Sun's most northerly position overhead at mid-summer, its apex will then be found to fall in the vicinity of the astronomical monument in the Temple of the Stars – often referred to as the Somerset Zodiac.

In England, the capstone itself, the eastern section is under the jurisdiction of Venus, the north of Mars, and the western section belongs to Earth itself, so all 'The Three Worlds' are represented. Consider the astrological implications, and think about the contributions these areas have made to Religion, Politics, Literature, World Discovery – everything connected with the world-wide development of our present culture, and you will see what a large proportion of it actually springs from the capstone, and that the most significant items were inspired by the people of that area. The New Renaissance, too, will come from the capstone, but expect to find some of its most able architects arriving via the north and north-west outlying squares.

But why do we double the pyramid? Because of the concept and the fact of that certain duality that runs through the whole history of mankind from the remote days of Atlantis on down to our own time. It discovers itself continually as we examine tradition, myth, symbol, and even recorded history itself, however distorted that may have become. The fundamental reference is to the people of the earth and the people of the sky, and to their relationship and communication existing between them. Had there been only one pyramid with one interesting corner (the Great Pyramid of stone at Giza) there would have been no real reason to consider it further. It could have been a mere coincidence, a chance relationship without any particular significance.

However, when it is possible to move the base of the pyramid southward to an important astronomical latitude, and when, by so doing, the apex falls out in the vicinity of the most sacred astronomical monument yet discovered on the face of the earth, and when, having done this, we are faced

with two parallel figures, one of which is a *corner*-stone of
Stone (earth) and the other an equally fantastic *cap*-stone of
Stars (the Zodiac), we may be excused for setting aside pre-
judices for a little space while we look into the matter.

Can there be any indications in the traditions of mankind
for belief that this relationship was deliberately planned and
executed, and for some reason great enough to justify the
effort, time and energy expended in the creation of such a
magnificent and complicated example of triangulation?

If two angles of a triangle are known the third can be
calculated. Therefore, if all three are known, to begin with,
and if one disappears (say, into the Atlantic Ocean), it can
always be located again. *The earthly triangle with the stone
pyramid corner-stone at Giza discloses the location of the
Lost Land.*

Has anyone ever stood at the centre of the Temple of the
Stars and sighted upward at an angle of 51 degrees 51
minutes 14.3 seconds? What would they see? What lies in that
direction – and at which hour of the day or night, and at what
time of year? Nothing at all, perhaps – or perhaps much.
However, if the earthly triangle refers to earthly localities,
why should not the heavenly triangle refer to some location in
the sky? We do not know. The mystery exists, but it has not
yet been fully explored or explained.

We have discovered through our second pyramid, that the
capstone lies in Britain. Let us now take another look at
Davidson and Aldersmith, who, in their writings, refer to
Colonel L. A. Waddell's book, *The Phoenician Origins of
Britons, Scots and Anglo-Saxons*.

They declare that Colonel Waddell 'shows the continuance
of a prevailing belief in a Divinely guided race known by the
name "Barats" or "Brits". This race is frequently represented
symbolically as a woman, Barat-Ana, ruling over the seas,
and accompanied by the sign of the "Sun of Righteousness",
a sun-circle encircling the St George and St Andrew crosses
(i.e., the Union Jack) . . .'

Colonel Waddell refers also to a representation on an early
pre-Christian coin of the Archangel Michael depicted 'with
eagle's wings and in other cases is symbolised by an eagle

upholding the symbol of the "Sun of Righteousness" while transfixing the serpent with its talons. The representation appears on an early Briton pre-Christian coin, and is an almost exact representation of what now figures as the Eagle of the United States of America. On the obverse side of the original seal is figured the symbol of the Stone Kingdom – a Pyramid with its Apex Stone (symbolic of Christ), containing the eye of Providence, suspended over it. . . .

'The Sun, Woman and Michael-Eagle symbols are, therefore mythologically and heraldically attached to the British race . . .'[67]

The cross, of course, is the ancient symbol of the four seasonal positions of the Great Bear, marking the solstices and the equinoxes. It is also the much maligned and often misused swastika, which the Nazis debased and reversed, but which began its existence as one of the holiest of Indo-European religious symbols.

The cult of the Bear and the Heavenly Tree (north pole of the sky), and of connection with the sky and its people, both of Heaven and of Earth, is much older than the 'Brits' or 'Barats' of Poseid. It has existed for an incredibly long time, and has been traced back 60,000 years. It was part of the religion of Neanderthal Man and still survives in its elements among certain people inhabiting parts of the far north of Siberia. The most interesting of the remains – and the most ancient – were discovered in a cave, high in the Alps. There were found ritually piled up bear skulls, and others that had been ceremonially encased in small stone chambers.

The Bear People are indeed very old. They became, in fact, symbolic of earth man, and the designation of the Arthur as 'Chief of the Bear Folk' places him in direct line of the oldest tradition in the world, showing him to be identical with the leader of that line of descent symbolised by the Earthly Brother in all the twin-symbols throughout the world – the earthly or younger brother who supplants, sometimes by subterfuge or violence, his elder or heaven-born twin, and usurps his inheritance. And, in this latter connection, it should not be forgotten that this so-called usurpation is eventually justified, because it must and ought to happen.

Earth man must finally learn to manage his own affairs. His

various tribes and divisions must learn to live at peace among themselves. He must some day get off the leading strings, learn to do without the supervision and guidance of his elder brother. In short, he must grow up, assume the dignity and responsibility of adulthood. When he does this, then all the substance of the Earth will be his to use and to enjoy.

10.   Return of the Earth-Shaker

We foresaw a time when men, exultant in the technique of homicide, would rage so hotly over the world that every precious thing would be in danger. – The High Lama

The Sky People probably first came back to attempt the rehabilitation of the planet about 1,000 years after the sinking of Poseid. This would be around 8000 BC, approximately when the first settlements known to modern archaeologists were started at Jarmo and Starr Carr. As we have seen, contact was established with nomadic animal-man and the arts of Agriculture and Building began. The Dual System was established. The teachers from the sky then tended to withdraw and Man was left to a greater extent to make use of the instruction given him.

For several thousand years, in various parts of the world, people continued to tend their fields, build bigger and better houses, grow rich and contented. They were not really aggressive – there were some minor local skirmishes – but not real warfare. That was to come later with the arrival of the warrior aristocracy from the outside – from the periphery of the existing cultures – and it was to overrun the world.

Who were these warrior peoples? After Poseid sank, the survivors fled in all directions to get away from the swirling waters and chaotic conditions. They went northward, southward, eastward and westward. Some survivors were still in Britain; some in Europe. Others moved out to the Middle East and even farther afield to India. They all emigrated from one central point. As Perry points out: 'The men of the archaic civilisation were moving out in an ever widening circle, so to speak, until they had encompassed most of the world. . . .'[68]

However, some of those who escaped from Poseid were of a very different calibre, more civilised than the nomadic re-

128

fugees we have been discussing so far. They, too, escaped from the devastating effects of the flood that had drowned their homeland, and their one thought was to put as much distance as possible between them and the terrible desolation they had left behind. The difference between them and the other nomadic animal men was that they were able to take with them their horses and their chariots – *for they never lost the wheel*. And, they had a great deal more of the old Atlantean knowledge. Above all, they remained culturally intact. They split up, it is true, into different groups, but they each kept the traditions and retained their knowledge of how to handle horses and other equipment.

Eventually, after the passage of time, the Earth became more stable and climatic conditions grew better. These communities had continued, biding their time, on the fringe of the agricultural communities. Tradition dies hard. They retained the memory – perhaps a half memory – handed down from father to son and then to grandson, of their 'Lost Island'. They wanted to find it again.

They also knew that all around them were rich, lush, agricultural countries ready for the picking. The occupants were leading a peaceful, but static farming life, and furthermore, did not possess the horse, far less know how to handle such an animal. Neither did they have the wheel.

So the warrior peoples began to move in. They overran their neighbouring agricultural communities, taking the women, the land and property. Although they invaded, looted and plundered, the warriors were not savage people of a primitive origin, but as Perry states: 'two important factors with regard to warrior aristocracies – they originate on the outskirts of highly developed civilisations and their place of origin shows traces of the past existence of a far higher degree of civilisation than they themselves possess. . . .'[69]

The warriors began to return from the periphery of existing cultures back to the centre. Due to the long aeons of time that had elapsed since their ancestors fled from Poseid, many of these warrior groups were not certain in which part of the world their 'Lost Island' lay. Various bands, therefore, went in different directions, even conquering the sub-continent of India in their search for the lost land.

One country, though, drew race after race of these warrior peoples to its shores like an irresistible magnet. One area was always defending itself against the invader. Which land was this? What country today has the blood of Vikings, Danes, Saxons, Teutons, Celts, the Belgae, the Beaker People and others, coursing in the veins of its people? Why, we may well ask, were these warrior peoples so persistently drawn to these islands – the so-called backward savage land of Ancient Britain? No army wants to cross the seas to invade such a land without a very good reason.

The answer is that these were the Islands of the Blest, the Land of the Hyperboreans, the legendary place where the stars had fallen from Heaven and where the gods danced in circles.

It is interesting to note that Mrs Maltwood mentions the national oath of the Celts as being: 'If we observe not this engagement may the sky fall upon us', and adds, 'Now in "Tain Bo Cauilgne" of the Book of Leinster (12th century manuscript) we find: "Heaven is above, and earth beneath us. Unless the sky shall fall with its showers of stars on the ground where we are camped . . . we shall not give ground." ' As Mrs Maltwood points out, 'The survival of a peculiar oath-formula for more than a thousand years, and its reappearance after being first heard of among the Celts of mid-Europe, in a mythical romance of Ireland is certainly most curious.'[70]

The Celts and the other warrior peoples were coming back to the remaining portion of the home of their ancestors – to Britain – the surviving connection with the drowned Poseid.

And what about this passage from Blavatsky, with especial reference to a zodiacal correspondence, to which we shall return in a moment?

'Every astronomer – not to speak of Occultists and Astrologers – knows that, figuratively speaking . . . the Milky Way and also the path of the Sun to the tropics of Cancer and Capricorn, as well as the Circles of the Sidereal or Tropical Year, were always called "Serpents" in the allegorical and mystical phraseology of the Adepts.

'Thus cosmically, as well as metaphorically, Poseidon is a "Dragon" – the Dragon "Chozzar, called by the profane Neptune" according to the Peratae Gnostics, the "Good and

Perfect Serpent", the Messiah of the Naaseni, whose symbol in Heaven is Draco.'[71]

Here we find not only one but a veritable basketful of interesting connections, Lord Dan was, symbolically, a Horse. He was also, symbolically, a Dragon. Have we here the source of the right of certain effigy horses, among people whose religion revolved around the god, to resemble dragons?

Is this a further welding together of ideas to support the presence of an artificial mound called Dragon Hill very near the great White Horse effigy at Uffington? Remember, too, that the god Poseidon is connected not only with water, but with both the Horse and the Dragon. And the White Horse at Uffington – symbol of Man – has the appearance of a Dragon!

We recall also, that at Dragon Hill, says tradition, lies buried Uther Pen-Dragon (whose name means Dragon's Head), who was the father of the first Arthur.

In the Somerset Zodiac we find, representing the Sign of Sagittarius, the Archer – a horseman and his horse. Maltwood equates the horseman with Hercules, because of the position of the stars. But Hercules is a zodiacal hero, with his twelve labours and his lion's skin. And King Arthur is his hyperborean counterpart.

From every direction the threads of association come together in the south and west of England, where wave after wave of the same root culture overlap and intermingle.

In the Temple of the Stars in Somerset, the head of the Giant Orion is called Dundon Hill. As Maltwood points out in her book, this combination of syllables means Castle of Wisdom, *Dun* Castle – *Don* Wisdom. It is not too difficult to see in this change of meaning, or shift of emphasis, the old central European Godword used by those Aryan-speaking peoples who moved out eastward, southward and westward, with their unique gifts to civilisation. Charles Seltman enumerates these: 'Wheeled vehicles, the art of producing wheel-made pottery, the horse, and their chief god – himself apt to be equine – Poseidon.'[72]

It is the *last syllable* in this word, Poseidon, which is of special interest. Don or Dan was the name of this god whose particular concern was water. Posei, or originally Potei, was his title, which meant something like Lord.

Seltman goes on to trace the origin of the word Zeus back
to this same god through certain variations in the spelling of
his name known to historians.

In modern times we associate Poseidon with the sea. The
orthodox explanation of this is that when the Greeks came
down from the north into what is now Greece, bringing with
them their Lord Dan (or Don) he was assimilated by other
peoples of the same racial and linguistic stock who had taken
to the sea. However, questions come to mind in connection
with all this, particularly, if one is interested in the myths and
stories about Atlantis.

Was not that last Atlantean island called Poseid (or Poseidonis)?

The civilisation we call our own today was born in the
Aegean, but the people who developed its essential forms, its
philosophy, its drama, and its sciences, were those children of
the 'Earth-Shaker' Potei-Don. They came into the settled,
well-fed, comfortable agricultural areas, and, quite literally,
put wheels under them.

The usual form of religion in the agricultural city states
was the old original worship of the Earth Mother. Caverns
were venerated. Artificial caves were constructed as places of
worship. Votive offerings were poured into or placed in pits
dug in the earth, after the manner of similar Neolithic practices unearthed, for instance, at Stonehenge, where holes have
been found containing sacrificial offerings. The earth, as
mother and nourisher of us all was venerated above all other
conceptions of deity.

Even in Egypt, where an early bringer of civilisation came
to be worshipped as a god, he was thought of as being unable
to return from the other world, and it was through his priestesses (represented by Isis, and Nephthys, the wife of his
brother, Seth), that his spirit was enabled to manifest itself
in the growing of the corn.

Potei-Don, or Poseidon, to give him his later and more
conveniently familiar name, was virile, male, and aggressive.
He was the 'Earth-Shaker'. Seltman described him: 'Thus
"Potei-Dan" or Zan, if he was the sky was the producer of
thunder. And at times he was a horse – not any horse, but
"HORSE" – an untameable stallion whose hooves thunder

across the wide grass-lands: one of the most dangerous of all creatures, and great in strength. Do we not as good Aryans still use him as a measure of "horse power"? And what can shake the earth better than the wild herd of stallions, mares, and foals in a stampede? When men have with infinite patience trained and reined them, there may come one day the cavalry charge or the massed onrush of battle-chariots, and once more the earth is shaken.

'In Homer, time and again, the favourite title given to Poseidon is "Earth-Shaker", for, by way of the charging stallion and the wild galloping herd, the divine "Horse" had become the god who made earthquakes. . . .'[73] The Aegean people, who did not have or remember the horse, had assigned his powers to the Bull, the Heavenly symbol of mankind's earthly regeneration.

The Earth Mother was considered to be his wife, but the system was patriarchal, whereas the religious life of the agricultural civilisations was still rooted in Neolithic matriarchy. There was a simple, practical and historical reason for this. In the beginning, agriculture was women's work. It was the women who tended the garden plots and carried on the primitive forms of hoe-culture. The coming of the plough began to change all this. Men took over a department of life which, always before, had been in the female realm. The same thing happened when the potter's wheel appeared upon the scene. Men took over the making of pottery, and industry, as we have come to know it, was born.

War, among the agriculturists, was confined to defensive manoeuvres of seasonal skirmishes with neighbours involving some attractive piece of arable countryside. Occasionally, the king of some city would set out and vanquish one of his neighbours, but it is doubtful if such forays would have stood inspection as really professional military operations.

Although the Indo-Europeans were credited with being warriors, and strictly must be classed as 'warriors' returning from the periphery to loot', they were probably no more professional. Their one deciding factor of superiority lay in their possession of the horse and wheeled vehicles.

The clashes between these two different types of civilisation set in motion the development of what is now called the Art of War. And wherever the more competent invaders from the north went, they absorbed or destroyed the more static civilisations. And wherever they went, the Mother Goddess gave way to the Horse and his Lord.

The Aegean civilisation stemmed from Crete and was centred there. Apparently it was well established when the inhabitants of the Nile Valley were persuaded to give up eating one another and improve their diet with the help of irrigation farming. Some authorities say the Cretan civilisation probably made large contributions to the Egyptian in its early stages. However, apart from trading extensively with everybody far and wide, the Cretans appear to have considered themselves to be superior and self-sufficient. Did they, perhaps, believe they had found and inherited 'The Island'?

If so, the rude shock came when the Mycenaean Greeks who had come originally out of the north, made one more move in their own eternal quest, and Knossos went up in flames. Here the conquest by the god of the north was so complete that a cave in Crete came to be pointed out as the birthplace of Zeus, who was our old friend, Potei-Don, under a slightly different (but linguistically legitimate) name, masquerading as his own 'younger brother'.

From this time onwards, further waves of immigrants came from the regions where the rivers bear the name of Don (Donau, Dneiper, Dneister, and even Don) and within about 400 years, the form of civilisation of which we are the heirs began to take shape in earnest.

And a point of interest is this: not only was this sort of thing going on in the Mediterranean world. Much the same things were happening in Mesopotamia, and in India, where other streams of immigrants had poured in from that same Middle-European nursery of the Sons of Poseidon.

Nor was the westward moving stream inactive. Far away in England, where the megalithic builders had gravitated, and where they had begun to transfer worship from the earth back to the sky, we see evidence of a great religious reformation. Religion suddenly comes up out of the ground, so to speak, and by about 1500 BC, we can discern the hand and the eye of an architect in the same traditions as those of Mycenae and Alalakh, and massive trilithons that forcibly recall the immensely older Gate of the Sun at Tiahuanaco.

The return of the Sons of the Lord of the Sea to an active participation in the world's affairs brought about the real beginnings of our civilisation, and however much we may deplore the faults of that civilisation, it is certainly neither static nor supine.

At about the same time the northerners began to move out into other areas, another people heard the call to go forth and seek a new homeland. Led by Abraham, they went first to Ur and from that city wandered on until they came to the Land of Canaan, and possessed it. Theirs was a much smaller migration, but they moved into direct contact with the incoming Indo-Europeans. Their ultimate contribution to the new amalgam took the form of religion and religious ideas. In time these ideas absorbed but did not entirely eradicate the ancient traditional forms.

In the complicated blendings of concepts that came to form the dominant religion of the Mediterranean and western branches of the migrations, the patronage of the seas was given back to the Mother of God, but there are curious survivals. Two very widely separated examples might bear mentioning.

To the north of Lebanon in the Turkish Hatay, at the mouth of the Orontes River, there is an almost forgotten site called al Mina, sometimes called in classical times Posideium. There, one object has survived untold centuries of abandonment, revival and natural destruction, which have all but obliterated this once thriving and important seaport. Sir Leonard Woolley tells us about it : 'A mile or so away to the north there stands on the edge of the lonely beach of black sand a solid whitewashed dome revered alike by Alauites, Moslems and Christians who from all the district round come on pilgrimage to burn incense at the common shrine: if you ask them who is the saint so honoured they will tell you "it is the Sheikh al Bahr", "the Lord of the Sea", and they will tell you nothing more. I like to think that the old sea-god whom the sailors of Alalakh knew 4,000 years ago, whom the Greeks, when they came, identified with their own Poseidon and named the port of their founding Posideium after him, is still, as the Sheikh al Bahr, ignorantly worshipped.'[74]

135

The other survival, up to the time of decimalisation of the British currency, was that trident in the hands of Britannia, which used to be seen on one side of the British penny. Alas, no longer!

This leads us to another question: The Indo-European-speaking, warrior groups who came out of their long isolation in Middle Europe and spread eastward, southward and westward, in their migrations, had been 'land-locked' for an unknown but certainly very long time. How was it then, that their Lord Don who 'became' Poseidon according to the scholars, had these three particular associations: weather, earthquakes, and above all, water?

His symbol was the trident, which later becomes the thunderbolt of Zeus, but remains to this day the three-pronged emblem of the sea. One would almost suppose its connection with lightning may have been a later development of the symbol – after it had been carried inland. By whom?

Admittedly, here we leave history behind a bit and go back to tradition. Could we say by 'refugees' from a country in the sea where there had been disastrous earthquakes, and from which Poseidon was remembered at first as a great king, then as a culture hero, and finally, honoured as a god, surrounded by the historical facts translated and transformed into his attributes?

If this did happen, then these people would have one of the best motives in the world for travelling onward until they found a land in which to settle that was about as far from any ocean as they could go.

Apparently, some people with the same sort of traditions, settled at first in the interior of Spain. These were the ancestors of some of the Beaker Folk (so named after the distinctive pottery they produced). However, it is interesting to see from maps of their migrations, that they moved into central Europe, very probably joining forces with extensions of their cousins who were already there, before turning westward and coming at last back to that part of the world most closely associated with their oldest traditions.

Perhaps, by that time they were looking for the Lost Island. Did they believe they had found it when they crossed the English Channel? Was the whole great outward movement of the Indo-European races prompted, at least in part, by some long-cherished and, finally, compulsive urge to seek the lost homeland of their origins? Orthodox opinion says they moved outward because of what are called 'population pressures'. This, it could be pointed out, is a very modern theory, evolved by people who think in terms of populations of a size and density unheard of in the world at the beginning of the second millennium BC.

According to legend, Poseidon had many children. If we can take the view that this means the people who worshipped Lord Don split up, in the course of history, into a number of different son-and-daughter groups, then we are able to look at mythology in a more intelligible light. In the Bible, when patriarchs are mentioned, even the most conservative of scholars in these days, does not hesitate to agree that these are family names. The long lives of the patriarchs then become reasonable lengths of time during which a certain family was important in the history of the nation. Mythology can be observed from the same point of view, and then it becomes very interesting, indeed.

In this connection, we can only wonder who the 'Sons of Poseidon' were who turned out to be winged or flying horses, because Pegasus was one of Poseidon's offspring. But, if we look briefly into the stories of the Mahabaratta, over in India, where some of the children of the Lord Don went to live, we find stories of flying cars! To people whose sole means of transport remained the horse, a flying means of transport would be explainable only as a horse with wings.

One of the Sons of Poseidon was a giant called Polyphemus. The blinding of Polyphemus by Odysseus, which was one of the harrowing events of his long tour, is a story familiar to everyone. But who was Polyphemus? Which of the peoples of the world will answer to the description suggested by the idea of considering the offspring of Poseidon to be groups of people who had survived the last Atlantean disaster?

There is one such group, and it is to be found in the Mediterranean area where the legend grew up – after, of course, the god had come back there with his people. This group is the pre-Dynastic Egyptians, whose tombs were found by Sir Flinders Petrie in such abundance at Abydos, where the Egyptians persistently worshipped Osiris. Osiris, they said, had taught them agriculture, the various arts of civilisation, and had persuaded them to give up cannibalism.

Polyphemus was a cannibal. The pre-Dynastic Egyptians had many practices in common with those sons of Poseidon of whom we have been speaking. Among the latter, cannibalism had become largely sacramental, as it may have been, for all we know, among the pre-Dynastic Egyptians. Later on, it became transferred to the consumption of the body (and/or blood) of a consecrated animal, but the mystery of the sacrificial flesh, human or animal, was definitely part of the picture among all these peoples. Perhaps it was a survival from the terrible memories of human destruction preserved in their traditions, which had become the foundations of their religion. However it originated, it came in somewhere and has remained as an everlasting and ineradicable impression. There are even modern survivals, albeit (may we say for ourselves?) at a figurative and symbolic level, and with highly spiritual overtones of which our remote ancestors may not have been capable.

Nevertheless, these Sons of Poseid – those distant warlike ancestors of people on earth now – were responsible for giving the initial impetus to our present-day civilisation. If they had not come out of their 'land-locked' isolation on the fringe of the existing agricultural states, we would not have had the wheel and the horse. Mankind, as a whole, would have continued its static agricultural life, which it had been carrying on for centuries, without any change.

The 'Earth-Shaker' gave mankind literally a shake-up and infused new vitality into its stagnant way of life. The Sons of Poseidon were, indeed, Men among mankind, and so were their descendants, Menes, Sargon, David, Solomon, Alexander and Hannibal.

The methods used by these warriors are abhorrent to many people living in these so-called civilised times. Their ways were expedient at mankind's stage of growth in those particular days. Drastic measures were necessary and, indeed, expected.

Strangely enough, the methods of the Warrior Aristocracy opened the way, so to speak, and made it possible for a da

Vinci, and later, a Telsa, to give mankind a new conception.

Everything happens in its own time. In the days of the Sons of Poseidon, the bulk of mankind was still very much in a primitive animal-like state and understood that way of living. Therefore, they had to be spoken to in the language of animals (at least to some degree), for communication to be effective.

In recent centuries and in our present era, most of Earth's people should have progressed beyond that animal stage. Today, different methods could be used and mankind ought, by now, to have grown out of the habit of using force against his fellows. It is obvious, with the example of two recent world wars of unparalleled dimensions within the short span of half a century, and the horrible threat of a third one with the added nuclear menace, that the lesson has not been properly assimilated, as yet.

11.   The Cities of the Plain

And he knew, too, . . . that this world was in peril . . . all was
about to be destroyed. – *Conway's thoughts*

Although there were probably men on Earth during the Age
of Cancer (9000 BC-6851 BC), Poseidon (Zeus) is the only one
that can be distinguished through legend and tradition, as
having become a culture hero, and, subsequently, worshipped
as a god in this era. He would have been remembered first as
Lord Don, King of Poseidonis (Poseid). Stories of that Lost
Island of the West – that became the underworld when it sank
into the ocean – would probably have centred around him as
their principal character.

Since he had reigned while Poseid was still a part of this
world, his connections were with water and with the sky, for
the legends would have included his communication with the
sky and with its people. This communication could have been
translated later on as a control of the phenomena associated
with the atmosphere, as bits of the legend were lost or became
distorted by subsequent interpretations. At any rate, Potei-
Don, when we find him in Middle Europe, has retained his
association with water, transferred, of course, to rivers and
springs, since the people had, at that time, no experience or
knowledge of the sea. Their ancestors had fled from the
ocean that had become, for them, a monstrous destroyer to
be feared.

Zeus is another name for Potei-Don. The intimate association between the two names is not obvious, but the derivation
of Zeus from Potei-Don through the form of Poseidon can
be shown to be logical within the workings of the Indo-
European language.

The birth story of Zeus is interesting in that it reveals the
ancient character of Zeus – Potei-Don. The father of Zeus was
Cronus, who represents Time. The story tells how, when
Rhea (or, Mother Nature) gave birth to her children, who

were the Titans, Cronus was jealous of them, although he was their father. One by one he swallowed them all as they appeared.

Clearly, time does swallow the gods of ancient peoples, as the world moves on, nations rise and disappear.

Rhea hit upon a scheme to outwit her husband when Zeus was born. She hid the baby in a cave in Crete, where he was cared for by the Nymphs, Adrasteia and Ida, who were daughters of the Cretan king. The sons of Cadmus, whom we call the Phoenicians, are credited with protecting him – and these were, of course, the worshippers of Barat-Ana.

In place of the infant, Rhea gave Cronus a stone wrapped up in swaddling clothes. This he swallowed, without investigating it, and the baby Zeus was saved.

Many scholars have wondered at this swallowing of the stone, but if one recalls what happened in the world after the people of Potei-Don became prominent and influential in it, the mystery dissolves. The whole Stone Age and its practices disappeared. Time swallowed it.

Cronus is also cognate with the astrological Saturn who is the divider of time and the Lord of Cycles. By Roman times he had taken on the aspect and functions of an agricultural divinity. He had become a 'working god and a vine-grower'.[75] Altars to Saturn had to be constructed of undressed stone upon which no tool had been laid. This injunction is reminiscent of the same rule which applied to altars to Jehovah who, in some respects, equates with Saturn. It brings us back, too, to that stone Rhea gave Cronus in substitution for their son.

Stone Age worship was predominantly the worship of the Earth Mother in a variety of forms representative of fertility and abundance. But Potei-Don or Zeus – was associated with the sky and all its phenomena. The Great Mother was his consort, but second to him in power and influence. The worship of Potei-Don transferred the focus of mankind's religious motives from the Earth as Mother to a being who was identified with the sky. In still another way the 'stone' was given figuratively, by the Great Mother Rhea, to Cronus, Time, who swallowed it. The Stone Age form of religion was superseded by the god of the sky.

141

The Great Pyramid's astrological chronology is oriented to the end of the Age of Gemini and the beginning of the Age of Taurus at 4699 BC. No individuals are recognisable, but all this time may be covered by the mythological activities of the gods associated with Zeus – Potei-Don, and Osiris. The age going out was the Age of Twins (Gemini) – the time during which the Men of Heaven supervised the affairs of mankind, and became thereby, the so-called gods.

Six hundred and ninety-five years after the beginning of the Age of Taurus (the Bull) the Bible tells us that earth man, as we know him, was 'made', that is, at 4004 BC. It is not until the Age of Taurus had continued since its inception in 4699 BC, for approximately 1,500 years that we come upon our first clearly recognisable individuals among mankind. Menes, in Egypt, who united the Upper and Lower Kingdoms and founded the First Dynasty, and, in Sumer, Emmerkar, Lugalbanda and Gilgamesh, who were among the first kings of the city of Erech. It is with their names that the recorded history of mankind begins again, and remains continuous up to the present time.

In the year 1862, a young Englishman named George Smith was first to discover the Babylonian story of the Flood during his study of clay tablets found in the library of King Ashurbanipal, who ruled in Babylon during the seventh century BC. Further discoveries and translations have enabled archaeologists to put together nearly the whole of the twelve poems, of which the Flood story is one. The hero of this epic is not a god, but a man named Gilgamesh. He was king of a city called Erech. This city stood at what was then the head of the Persian Gulf, between the Euphrates and the south fork of the Tigris. The rivers have since changed their channels, and the city now lies miles inland. The Persian Gulf silts up at present at the rate of about seventy-five feet a year, due to the tremendous amount of mud brought down by the two great rivers.

Gilgamesh, at the outset of his career, is portrayed as a somewhat overbearing monarch, besides being both a boisterous and irresponsible character. The citizens of Erech complained to their gods, and the Mother Goddess Aruru took clay and made Enkidu, who was a kind of wild, animal-man.

142

He lived with the animals until a courtesan of Erech tamed him and brought him to Gilgamesh. In the story, he does not want to attend a certain feast with Gilgamesh. He is shocked by the nature of the affair and bars Gilgamesh's way at the door. Gilgamesh is enraged by this interference and the two heroes wrestle together in the street. When Enkidu is about to overcome Gilgamesh, the latter suddenly gives up and the two become fast friends.

After a while they make a long journey to a cedar forest guarded by a terrible dragon, the Huwawa; kill it, and cut down its sacred tree. The many other adventures of these two friends, one 'made by the gods' and, therefore, associated with the sky, and the other, a man of earth, are too long and involved to consider here. It is this dragon story that interests us most directly.

Here, perhaps, for the first time, we find the elements of a plot that becomes very familiar to us as we look back through history: the dragon of the north and his sacred tree, which in all cases appear to be figures of the old polar constellation. Apparently, this group of stars which contained what was the Pole Star in those early times, Alpha Draconis, has always been known by names that have the same meaning as our word 'dragon'. The idea that the north pole of the sky is symbolically supported by a great tree is, apparently, as old as Man.

Why, then, slay the dragon who is 'guardian of the Land of the Living'?

The north celestial pole does not always remain in the same place. Due to a movement of the Earth's axis, the north celestial pole describes a circle over a very long period of time, and different stars appear close to the pole as the cycle proceeds.

When the dragon constellation seemed to move away from the polar position he could be thought of, in poetic terms, as having been slain, and, as in the case of the Sumerian epic, his tree cut down. That this act was credited to a Sumerian culture hero is a part of the psychology of a Heroic Age, during which all sorts of fantastic enterprises are attributed to the heroes. Heroic Ages have been pointed out to be phenomena associated with a kind of adolescent period in the growth of a civilisation. Dr Samuel Noah Kramer points out that Heroic Ages go along with 'national migrations', and further, that the migrating peoples have been in touch with the periphery of a more settled and highly developed civilisation prior to their movement inward toward its centres.[76]

Apparently, the pre-Sumerian culture in Mesopotamia had been developed by a people who came into the area from Persia. Semites moved in from the west and the two cultures mingled and gave rise to a 'peasant village culture'.[77] Then the Sumerians moved in from the west. Emmerkar, Lugalbanda and Gilgamesh were among their earliest kings, 'the second, third, and fifth rulers of the First Dynasty of Erech, which, according to the Sumerian sages, followed the First Dynasty of Kish, which in turn followed immediately upon the Flood.'[78] The beginning of all this goes back to approximately the time when Menes was uniting Upper and Lower Egypt. The movement toward large areas of unified civilisation had begun.

It was about 3000 BC that Gilgamesh was king of the city state of Erech. One of the neighbouring city states was Kish. Dr Kramer states that Kish 'according to Sumerian legendary lore had received the "kingship" from heaven immediately after the "flood" '.[79]

This flood could not have been the inundation calculated by the compilers of Genesis, and to which they attached much of the previous material borrowed from Babylonian sources concerning an earlier and probably more extensive disaster. The 'flood' mentioned in connection with the kingship of Kish seems more likely to have been the catastrophe or series of catastrophes, that occurred about 4000 BC.

At that time the whole of the Tigris and Euphrates area was invaded by the sea. A layer of mud containing marine animals was laid down, and, under Ur, the city that stood near the head of the Persian Gulf, that mud layer is still ten feet thick, after having been compressed under 6,000 years of subsequent deposits. At Kish, which lies south-east of Babylon, the layer is still eighteen inches deep. Archaeologists estimate the area covered by this flood must have been at least 100 miles wide and about 400 miles long.

This is by no means 'the whole world'. However, in other parts of the Earth there are evidences of catastrophic upheavals and geological displacements, all coinciding more or less closely with the early part of the Taurean Age, and centring around the period of about 4000 BC. The world was undergoing one of its cyclic periods of upheaval and change. The Alps and the Himalayas, and probably, the Andes, were pushing upward once more. Their added height brought about drastic changes in the pattern of world glaciation and the weather. The level of the sea rose and fell again. Mankind's precarious hold upon civilisation was seriously threatened, and in some places, at least, it seemed to the people that the end of their world had come.

From the stories that remain to us of that time, it is clear that 'Heaven' and the so-called gods took a hand in the affairs of mankind. They helped to restore civilisation and order. Kish, we hear, received its kingship from 'Heaven', and it is to this same period the compilers of Genesis, working from the Babylonian records, refer the creation of the second Adam.

The Babylonians were great borrowers of other people's literature and legends. They took the old stories and embroidered them, making them over to suit themselves, and often in such cases distortion appears. Separate incidents far apart in time are collapsed into one another and become one story. Something like this must have happened to the second Hebrew creation myth, for we know now, from archaeological evidence, that mankind existed in the world for a long time before the biblical date of the creation, 4004 BC. But, as we have seen, that date happened to coincide with a critical period in the history of the Earth. One wonders: Were that Adam and his people among the principal survivors of the catastrophes, and did the older traditions collapse around him afterwards, so that he came to be called The First Man by at least one nation? Was that particular Adam, perhaps, one of the earliest kings in some now lost Mesopotamian city state, which, like Kish (and probably more or less contemporary with it) received kingship 'from Heaven', got a fresh start, and re-established what was to become our own historical civilisation? This would certainly seem to be sufficient grounds for his being invested by his descendants with the attributes of The First Man.

Certainly, about 1,000 years later, we find the city states in Mesopotamia already well established and flourishing upon the remains of an agricultural village society directly beneath which lies this great expanse of a deep layer of mud and clay laid down by the invading ocean.

Emmerkar, Lugalbanda and Gilgamesh, are the names of three of the kings of the First Dynasty of Erech. Before them had come the dynasty of Kish, and before that, the flood. The dynasties of Kish and Erech established Sumer. From the time just after the flood until about 3000 BC, Kish appears to have been supreme. But, about the time that Menes was consolidating Upper and Lower Egypt, the kings of Erech began to become more powerful and influential, and we hear of Emmerkar, Lugalbanda and Gilgamesh.

From the time of Gilgamesh until about the middle of the third millennium BC, Sumer prospered. Then Semitic peoples appeared on the scene, moved into the area and conquered Kish. Marching on down the rivers they took over everything in their way, and came to Erech which they captured and held. Their leader was an extraordinary individual named Sargon. Before he died, nearly all of the Near East was under his rule. As Menes had done before him, he united a loose and often quarrelling group of little city states into the first semblance of a nation.

According to accounts handed down to us today, Sargon's mother was a lowly woman, and he did not know his father. His mother conceived him at Azupira-nu on the banks of the Euphrates. He was cast adrift on the river in a basket of rushes, and eventually retrieved by a man called Akki, who was an irrigation worker. Akki took the boy home and brought him up as his own son. He taught Sargon to be a gardener. In time, Sargon got a menial job in the royal service at the palace in Kish, and must have commended himself to his employers, as it is recorded that he was promoted to the post of cup-bearer, a very respected and sought-after position at court. He then found it possible to aspire for the throne itself and after conquering Erech, he founded a new capital for himself at Agade.

Sargon then had to contend with the Sumerian cities of the south, and succeeded in defeating Ur. He went on to conquer many lands, and, as C. J. Gadd relates, 'From the mountains of Elam to the Phoenician coast his rule was spread by a succession of campaigns and he is even said to have extended his sway over the distant Kaptura, which should be the island of "Crete".'[80]

The conqueror divided up his vast empire between his heirs, the 'sons of his palace'. However, his long reign of triumph and glory ended with the whole of the empire in revolt, primarily because it was said he violated the holy city of Babylon. His own troops bound Sargon in a ditch and destroyed him.

Sargon was known as 'King of the Land and King of Universal Dominion'. He was also a priest-king, although at the same time one of the earliest known warrior kings. *He was a very early outstanding example of the ferment that was coming upon the world.*

The city he founded was called Agade. This is a name that immediately brings to mind the name of another city associated with much tradition and speculation – the city of the north – Agharti. Did Sargon know of, or have some connection with the people of Agharti who, tradition says, kept and preserved the ancient records of the world, going back for tens of thousands of years? No one knows, today, where *either* of these cities were or are. Rumour has it that Agharti is somewhere in, or to the northward of, what is now Tibet. Sargon's Agade was somewhere in the area watered and fed by the two great rivers, Tigris and Euphrates. If it can be found and explored by the archaeologists, perhaps another chapter in the history of mankind will come into view.

Certainly, Sargon was a remarkable and unusual Man. The stories associated with his birth resemble those of other remarkable Men and will bear looking into.

Agade continued for about 100 years. Barbarians out of the east, a savage people called the Guti, suddenly descended upon Sumer, and the destruction was terrible. The Sumerian records call them 'a people which brooks no controls'; 'it covered the earth like the locust'.[81] The great and beautiful city King Naram-Sin had inherited from his grandfather, Sargon, fell, and there was famine in Sumer. A scribe recorded the devastation on a clay tablet which archaeologists have translated. From his description there would seem to be little room to wonder that the city of Sargon has never yet been found.

12. Revival of Monotheism

It could hardly be expected that one man unaided should uproot permanently the habits and tradition of an epoch. — *The High Lama*

About the middle of the eighteenth century the general European attitude towards so-called primitive peoples began to undergo a reversal. The new outlook began with a Frenchman, Jean Jacques Rousseau, who introduced to the philosophical world the concept of the 'noble savage', and who proposed that simple, uncomplicated almost animal existence was the natural, and therefore most desirable, state, from which mankind had somehow fallen into degeneracies of civilisation. Rousseau gained many followers and his ideas are still clearly visible in the aims of numerous Utopian groups and other world-mending organisations.

The new point of view played a large part in the abolition of slavery, and tribes of primitives became objects of serious study, instead of candidates for exploitation or immediate extermination. Out of this interest came modern anthropology and ethnology as we know them today. Highly perceptive, well-qualified men and women began to go and live among the less civilised peoples of the world, and to study not only the outward aspects of their ways of life, but the beliefs, the morals and ethical codes that underlie, and indeed, give strength, as well as continuity, to all the numerous varieties of local convention and behaviour.

The belief is still widely held among civilised people that primitive mankind was (or is) a 'simple child of nature', with the mentality and reactions of a very young child. According to this view, mankind's religious ideas are supposed to have originated in fanciful explanations of phenomena encountered in the environment, and to have developed, via a process of Darwinian evolution, slowly and somewhat painfully, from a level of unsophisticated and, at least, partly subconscious

149

fantasy, to the grand and glorious concept of a single Universal Divinity with which the more adult mind of modern Man is blessed. In the twentieth century, this belief is undergoing some rapid and surprising revision, as anthropologists and ethnologists, patiently research and unravel the workings of the primitive mind.

Entities once mistaken for gods are frequently found to resemble much more closely the civilised person's acceptances of patron saints, or angels of either the good or bad variety. At one time all such entities were translated indiscriminately as gods, and the idea that so-called polytheistic systems might possess at least as many levels as the Hierarchies of Heaven did not, apparently, occur to the investigators. Now, however, the tables are beginning to turn. Intensive study of these primitive peoples who have, somehow, remained uninfluenced by the stream of progress, has revealed as a matter of hard fact that mankind, before civilisation sets in, is a Monotheist. The firm belief in one Supreme Creator is the indisputable and original heritage of all mankind, no matter how many other lesser entities came to be accepted as administrators of this world and its weather. The notion that civilised mankind achieved the concept of Monotheism, perhaps, as one of the consequences of his growing in understanding, or through the agency of his developing and maturing mind, has had to be given up, and replaced by more sobering consideration.

Civilisation, with its growing emphasis upon power and authority over larger and still larger groups, and increasing control of mankind by mankind in the absence of direct intervention or direction from any other source, permitted Polytheism to arise. Heroic men and women, dimly remembered from ancient times, were elevated to positions of importance in the other world that was supposed to be interested in this one – and that other world became an immaterial realm, associated partly with the sky and partly with an underworld that had become equally immaterial. Thus, this hazy heaven (which even modern Man has largely inherited) gradually became populated with numerous personages who had achieved divinity or semi-divinity, and, whose immediate control of affairs and events in this world, superseded and finally obliterated the original idea, of the one Supreme Creator and Preserver of us all.

Civilised mankind, therefore, had to rediscover his Monotheism. This rediscovery, besides the subsequent refinement and improvement of the concept, has been the work of individual Men. They were Men with the stamp of inspiration plain upon them, and indeed, the greatest among them did not hesitate to claim to have conversed with the Almighty Himself, so profound was the effect of the impressions they received. Whether or not they did actually meet the Supreme Spirit face to face is, at this writing, a matter for personal theological decision. The effect is the same as if they did, for the idea took root again among mankind, for it grew and has developed into interesting forms. Along with it there returned something of the old certainty of 'ever present help in time of trouble' for all mankind on earth, instead of for one small group in opposition to another. Although this lesser idea still persists, it is steadily losing ground and showing signs of eventually being supplanted by the wider concept.

When civilised mankind rediscovered Monotheism, the idea did not arrive in any highly developed or universal form. Thousands of years passed before the concept matured and expanded sufficiently for any significant part of mankind to grasp, and to retain the archetypal image of one, Universal Supreme Being. The only possible exceptions were a few isolated individuals whose realisation died with them, and some of the esoteric groups or mystery schools which taught the wider conception in secret, and under vows of concealment from the rest of the world. Mental and emotional horizons were far too limited to contain such a thought, and many steps had to be taken before it could find widespread acceptance.

The beginnings were small and at first obscure, as all beginnings must be. The first Man to whom the revelation came, according to available records, rejected the thinking of his time, which postulated a number of gods and godlings for each group of families, and initiated the first step towards mankind's appreciation of the cosmic ideal. His realisation that all the families of his kindred had, in fact, but one deity who must be the supreme authority for them, set him and his relatives apart from their contemporaries. It is doubtful if this strange, new attitude could have survived in the environment in which it arose. Traditional thinking, and above all, feeling, might well have overwhelmed it.

However, the custodian of this radical notion foresaw what such a departure could mean to the future of a group like the one of which he was the patriarch, and we are informed that his god told him that his people would become a great nation, if he went away from the land of his fathers, and settled in another place, amongst strangers, who would have, of course, far less influence upon the thinking of his people. Therefore, in obedience to what he considered a divine command, he gathered the families together and set out upon a journey which was, in the end, to change the theology of a major portion of the world.

The name of this extraordinary Man was, at first, Abram (the spelling was later changed to Abraham). It means, in Hebrew, 'father is high', and his descendants are the Israelites. A great mass of tradition gathered around his name and memory, as always happens to such influential Men, but it has been clearly determined that the city of his fathers was Haran. In Genesis 11, you will find his genealogy, and archaeologists have uncovered the interesting fact that most of the names of his ancestors were actually the names of cities in the north-western part of Mesopotamia, in the plain of Aran. The time in which he lived was the nineteenth century BC – a time almost as long before the birth of Jesus, as our time is after that event – more than six centuries before Moses led the Exodus out of the land of Egypt.

During all that time, the children of Abraham were custodians of the New Thought of their age, and its realisation grew along with them, as they struggled against the established disorder of the period and became, as was promised at the beginning, an important nation. It was one of their number born in captivity in Egypt, who achieved the next step upward and outward for mankind.

Scholars continue to dispute with one another about the derivation of the name of Moses. Some prefer to associate it with the Egyptian word *māshāh* meaning 'one who draws', referring to the story that the Egyptian princess drew him out of the waters of the Nile. Others (and they represent a small majority) recommend the Egyptian word *mes(u)*, which means 'child' or 'son of', and is a form common to many Egyptian names.

The multitude of detail that has come down to us about this great lawgiver and prophet, is available to anyone, in the Bible and elsewhere. However, certain aspects of the picture are important to our own tale. One of these is the great revelation that came to Moses and its ultimate consequences in the history of Monotheism, for it was Moses who first broke the bounds of the old horizon laid down by Abraham, and who released religious thinking into a new, more active, and more comprehensive field.

'Moses was the first historic individual who can be said to have welded the Israelite clans into a whole.'[82] The promise held from the days of Abraham was at last to be fulfilled, but not without great effort, and not without opposition and many setbacks.

Historians now agree, substantially, upon an approximate but still closely accurate date for the Exodus: about 1290 BC, which fell during the reign of Ramesses II. This was the Pharaoh who was possessed by such a strong enthusiasm for building, and who so shamelessly erased the names of former builders from their monuments in order to inscribe his own. Beyond any reasonable doubt it was this ambitious man who impressed the immigrant Israelites residing in the land of Goshen (a fertile plateau between the east branch of the Nile and the northern end of the Red Sea) into labour gangs and employed them in his undertakings. Pictures of them at work making his 'bricks without straw' are to be found in tombs of the period, in which Semitic workmen are shown engaged in this and associated tasks, under the ever watchful eyes of their African overseers who hold the corrective baton 'at the ready' to punish shirkers and slackers.

It was one of these hated overseers that Moses smote and killed when he found the man mistreating an Israelite. In consequence of this rash action, Moses was forced to leave the country until such time as the affair could be quieted and forgiven, if not forgotten. Not even his relatively high position could have protected him from the law. He sought and found sanctuary with some distant kinsmen of his who were descendants of one of Abraham's wives, whose name, Keturah, means 'incense'. It is interesting to observe that these Midianites lived in the northern part of Arabia. Part of the territory they occupied lay across the caravan route from Yemen to Egypt and Syria. This is the route that led from Arabia Felix, a land full of 'much spices', a part of which was later to become the country of the Queen of Sheba, who visited Solomon. The Midianites who lived in that part of the world which is now Saudi Arabia, or the main Arabian peninsula, were connected with the trade between Yemen and the Mediterranean world of the time. They were caravaners. The *Encyclopaedia Britannica* says they were called 'incense men'. They also dealt in gold and very possibly copper, which was already being mined heavily in the wind-cut valleys of Arabia.

The man with whom Moses went to live was a pastoral Midianite, settled near the southern end of the Sinai peninsula. His name was Jethro and he was a priest of a god named something like Yahweh, whose principal habitation was one of the local mountains known in one language as Horeb, and in another language as Sinai – at least, this was how it seemed to the Midianites at that time. Jethro was a very wise and learned man. His Midianite connections must have brought him information from most of the then known world, and his wisdom in practical affairs is apparent in the wise counsel he gave to Moses later on, after the Exodus, when Moses fell into difficulty with administrative affairs. Researchers are coming more and more to realise that Moses, while tending the flocks of Jethro, had a great opportunity to learn many things that had nothing whatever to do with counting sheep.

It was during this period that Moses beheld the 'vision' of the burning bush on Sinai (Horeb), and this is where the god of Jethro identified himself as: 'the God of thy father, the God of Abraham, and God of Isaac, and the God of Jacob.'[83] Moses, after not a few objections, finally accepted the divine command to return to Egypt, gather together the Israelites, and bring them back to Sinai.

Some time before this incident, Moses had married Zipporah, one of the daughters of Jethro. We see him setting out upon his mission, after having been assured that 'all the men are dead which sought thy life'.[84] (In Egypt, and in reference to the incident of the overseer.) And so began the second and greater chapter in the history of the rediscovery of Monotheism. Moses did not live to enter the Promised Land, but, although no direct mention of it is made in the biblical account, the Israelites continued to have available to them the advice of his adviser and probable teacher, Jethro. At the invitation of Moses, Jethro and his clan moved on with the liberated Israelites (and with the God of the mountain who went with Moses and his people) and took up new residence in southern Judaea.

There were two very fundamental differences between the Mosaic God and the religions already existing in Canaan. These were: (1) the exclusive worship of Yahweh, and no other god, and (2) that Hebrew has no term for 'goddess'. Yahweh had no consort, no female counterpart. He could and did exist without dependence of any kind upon the Earth or any symbol thereof. Like the more Ancient Egyptian Aton (who later got himself lost in a wilderness of lesser administrative aspects of his functions), the God of Moses was conceived as being one single entity, alone, and without a second. This was a distinct and direct break with the other religions of the time, who still held to the Mother Goddesses which they had inherited from the old Stone Age.

There was a tendency as time went on to mingle the practices of these older religions with the worship of Yahweh, and it was this backward-looking tendency the prophets militated against and managed, in the end, to curb.

One of these prophets, Amos, achieved a vision that was far in advance of the thinking of his time, and it had a profound effect upon the history of Monotheism. Until the ninth century BC, the God of Moses, although implicitly much more, had remained, to all intents and purposes, the national god of the Israelites, inspiring them to both political and racial solidarity, as well as patriotism. Amos provided the next great step toward a new horizon. He thought of Yahweh and portrayed him as a Universal Lord, who was not only a leader of his own chosen people, but creator of the Earth, the sky, and even of the stars themselves; in short, the Universe. It was the first great cosmic concept. To this, Amos added an emphasis upon the importance of a righteous life, rather than sacrifice, in order to gain the favour of God. Thus, two more sturdy and enduring props were added to the foundation of mankind's monotheistic theology, and a new, wider circle was established for the mind of mankind to explore. It became possible for the people of Earth to consider themselves in an entirely new set of relationships, not only to family and tribal groups, but to nations, the entire world and to the Universe.

Jeremiah, who followed Amos, attempted to add to this new step ethical concepts beyond the capacity of his time. He understood the teachings of Amos in a new and different light, comprehending that external observances were not fundamental, but, in reality, only the outward effect achieved by a wide practice of individual and personal realisation. It was Jeremiah who placed individual responsibility before mankind as a first necessity for what the modern Christian Church calls the reception of Grace. He recognised that the time was at hand for the establishment of a new covenant, and because the sense of responsibility involves the emotions first of all, his new covenant was to be of the heart, and was not concerned merely with the life of the body in the chemical world.

The consequence of this idea, and in a way the other side of its coin, is the very idea of the freedom of the individual which plays such an important part in the thinking of our own era. From the time of Jeremiah and Ezekiel, who was, in a way, his student and disciple, at least a part of mankind on Earth was given the opportunity to look forward to his own salvation as coming from himself, via his own actions, instead of an inherited beneficence to which he was somehow entitled by the sanctity of his ancestors.

The revelation of Jeremiah and Ezekiel came too late to save the political situation of the time. The temple was finally destroyed in 586 BC. The people of Yahweh went into yet another exile, and out of this was born the concept of the long-suffering servant, which fell, in time, into the degraded and degrading idea of servitude for spiritual gain. The idea of suffering vicariously in this world in order to gain the rewards of the next, has not even yet been eradicated from the emotional reactions of mankind.

Five hundred years after the time of Jeremiah a voice cried in the wilderness. 'There was a man sent from God, whose name was John.'[85] It was his voice that revived the disrupted line of prophetic tradition. Following immediately after him there came the Nazarene, Jesus, his cousin, who was to set half the world on fire with the old, forgotten hope of reconciliation and understanding, and ultimately communication, between mankind and his Cosmic Source.

It was this same Jesus who was cousin to the British Arthur who, although the last of his traditional line, still bore witness to the oldest religious inheritance of mankind in this world – the ancient observances belonging to the polar constellations, the Dragon, the Bear, and the Eagle, and on Earth to those who raised up mighty stones.

The contributions Jesus of Nazareth made to the growth and spread of Monotheism are well enough known to all. He restored the grand prophetic tradition, and like most of the prophets he was suspected of heresy, at least in some quarters, in his own time. His followers made what they could of his teachings, and branched off in a variety of differing directions. After 2,000 years the result of their efforts is still a live and growing factor in the world's affairs, and where the future will take the many forms of Christianity, no man can say.

Jesus advanced the cause of Monotheism by reiterating the ideas first expressed by Jeremiah, and later by his pupil Ezekiel. He presented them again with such force that they have never since been forgotten by mankind. Jeremiah arrived on the scene a little too late to save his nation from the fate that had been brewing for it a long time. It is still too difficult to determine just what the ultimate effect of the arrival of Jesus upon the Judaeo-Roman scene, at the particular time when he appeared, will be. The fact remains that he left the way open for the appearance of the next great prophet in a direct line through the old tradition. That prophet appeared among another group of people descended from the children of Abraham, and the world has yet to deal with the constantly accumulating results of his teaching.

It would seem to be quite clear from the content of the gospels that Jesus originally thought of his mission in terms of his being a messenger to the descendants of Abraham, in particular to that segment of them among whom he was born. It was only with the greatest reluctance and at the insistence of his disciples, that he crossed the Jordan and talked to Gentiles. His vision may have provided him with some idea of what would happen if he did. At any rate, it was the Gentile nations who adopted a form of his teachings not entirely pleasing to Simon Peter (who was the Rock upon whom Jesus hoped to found his Church), and they gave the world the variety of faiths we know today as Christianity.

The theme of personal responsibility and its corollary, the possibility of personal and intimate communication with the one Supreme Deity was the essence of the message of Jesus, as it was the foundation of Jeremiah's earlier and unsuccessful realisation. To Jeremiah's ideal, Jesus added the concept of a mediator, himself. To some extent, this has resulted only in the sort of development Jethro, the father-in-law of Moses, foresaw when he observed Moses attempting to judge all the affairs of the Israelites in the name of his God.

'And it came to pass on the morrow, that Moses sat to judge the people: and the people stood by Moses from the morning unto the evening.

'And when Moses' father-in-law saw all that he did to the people, he said, What is this thing that thou doest to the people? Why sittest thou thyself alone, and all the people stand by thee from morning until even?

'And Moses said unto his father-in-law, Because the people come unto me to enquire of God:

'When they have a matter, they come unto me: and I judge between one and another, and I do make them know the statutes of God, and his laws.

'And Moses' father-in-law said unto him, The thing that thou doest is not good.

'Thou wilt surely wear away, both thou and this people

that is with thee: for this thing is too heavy for thee: thou art not able to perform it thyself alone.'

Exodus xviii, 13-18.

Jesus, for reasons of his own, and because of his own realisation of himself, thought otherwise in his own case. However, the still unanswered question is: was he able to communicate that realisation to other people? Hopefully, he is reported to have said: 'Greater things than these shall ye do after me.' The world, sad to say, is still reluctant to accept any evidence of such activity when it appears, even in much lesser instances than those to which Jesus was making his comparisons when he spoke to his followers.

Moses sought to be a mediator between the mundane affairs of his people and his God. Jethro pointed out to him the folly of such a course of action. Out of the system devised throughout the following centuries, and based upon the suggestion of Jethro, there grew up the body of that Law which Jesus said he had come not to destroy but to fulfil.

Most of the religious practices and most of the ideas observed in Christianity today, in any form, are manifestly not the practices or the ideas observed by Jesus. They are, on the contrary, the outgrowth of many interpretations and much compromise. The legitimacy of this development cannot be called into question. Any system must be capable of growth and change, if it is to survive in a world of change and evolutionary expansion. Times change, and with them customs, religious and otherwise. Here we are merely cataloguing the efforts of certain Men and observing the more obvious results.

One of the results of the Nazarene's campaign has been that he is now deified and made into a segment of a triune divinity worshipped by most of his professed followers in the twentieth century after his birth. Jesus is now God to much of the world's population.

Because of this fusion of persons and the appearance of Trinitarian doctrine, the main stream of monotheistic religious thought was turned aside from a long-established course. It remained for another descendant of Abraham, an Arabian this time, to bring it back again, and the Man who said firmly, for all to hear, There is no God but God, was a well-born but humbly situated camel driver who had married well.

If people today think about Arabia at all, they usually picture it as a sea of sand punctuated by oil-wells and inhabited by exotic figures hooded and burnoused against the sun. This image is not quite true, even now, and in the days of Solomon it would have been even farther out of focus. Earlier than that, by another thousand years or so, such a picture of desolation would hardly fit at all. The climate of Lesser Asia has changed almost unbelievably, and most of the change is undoubtedly due to the depredations of mankind and of his domesticated animal friend, the all-devouring goat. Together they have managed to denude the area of its once towering stand of timber and other important vegetation. Mankind did not spare the cedars, and his millions (literally) of goats nearly finished off such lesser verdure as might have survived their masters' unscientific lumbering operations.

In the days of its glory, Arabia produced a definite type of mankind, which anthropologists assume to be indigenous to the area. One group claims descent from Shem, and another from Ishmael. There has been some infiltration from North Africa of other peoples, but on the whole, anthropologists now concede that Arabia, particularly the southern part once called Arabia Felix, may well have been the birthplace of the Semitic peoples. The physical and mental superiority of these people of Araby has excited the wonder of investigators, while, at the same time, their general indifference to large-scale organisation and inborn resistance to regimentation appears as a serious defect to the European mind, which interprets this characteristic as 'an incapacity for combined action'. The true Arab is an individualist, and so is his God.

This, then, was the heritage of the Prophet who is known in the western world as Mahomet. He was born about AD 569, into a family of the tribe of Koreish, and his name, Ahmad (or Muhammad) means 'the praised', in Arabic, and 'the desired' in Hebrew.

His accomplishments are not as well appreciated as they might be among the Christian nations. This unfortunate attitude can be traced largely to the hostility which developed between the two religious groups, each of which set out to make its own faith the dominant belief of the world. However, all this difficulty aside, the Christian world owes a debt of gratitude to Mahomet and his followers that can hardly be repaid, and the cause for that gratitude lies in the realms of the mind, in the spheres of philosophy, medicine and science.

This is an aspect of history too often played down by Christian writers on the subject. If one peers past their prejudices and considers the situation with a more impartial eye, the cold fact remains that very little of the philosophy which formed the basis of the Renaissance would have survived its Grecian eclipse, had it not been for the tireless activities of the scholars of Islam. They recorded and kept it alive between the ninth and the middle of the twelfth centuries, when Europe was no fit home for either philosophy or scientific enquiry. Mahomet reawakened the Arabian mind, and the works of the Greek philosophers, astronomers and mathematicians, found refuge and sanctuary among Arabian thinkers. When the mind of Europe began to struggle up out of its thousand years of darkness, it was to the writings of Islam's philosophers and scholars, and to the works they had preserved, that it turned for its enlightenment.

None of this would have happened without the teachings of Mahomet. At one time, long before his birth, a literature and much learning had flourished in Arabia, but the course of history had changed in such a way that most of this had been lost or reduced to oral tradition. The art of Writing, while not entirely lost, was not thought much of, either. It is even said that the Prophet himself could neither read nor write — as, indeed, many of his contemporaries could not. In all likelihood, however, he knew something of the art.

Be that as it may, the very first of the revelations which were to accumulate and to become the Holy Koran of Islam struck a blow at the roots of this contempt for literacy. It begins with a command to 'Read in the name of thy Lord who creates . . .' and it exalts the use of the pen. The followers of the Prophet took this injunction to heart and preserved not only their own Holy Book but a whole world of knowledge, adding to the store from their fertile intellects as they went along.

Islam made another indirect contribution to the evolution of western European ideas, and it may yet prove to be of more importance than is generally realised. The Sons of the Prophet have bolstered and upheld with unswervable determination the monotheistic concept of universal deity in a very pure and undiluted form. 'There is no God but God' was the cry of Islam that rang in European ears and disturbed even the disputations of Trinitarian theologians in their councils. On the whole, mankind has not yet achieved a completely clear or definite vision of the unqualified monotheistic ideal. At the risk of his very life, the Prophet Mahomet cut through all disagreements with one short, unequivocal statement, and Islam assumed its role of militant custodian of the ancient Semitic inspiration of One, Supreme Lord of the Universe, who is without a second. The sword of the mind cut through the tangled knot of superstition and speculation, and for at least a little while the divine vision stood clarified and plain for all to see who could bear to look.

13. The Warrior and the Builder

Perhaps the exhaustion of the passions is the beginning of wisdom, if you care to alter the proverb. – *Conway*

King Solomon has been called the greatest and wisest among men. Yet, unlike so many well-known historical figures – Osiris, Krishna, Sargon, Moses, to name a few – there is apparently no mystery connected with his birth and ancestry. His father, David, although a remarkable man, is clearly stated to have been the youngest son of Jesse, who lived in the little town of Bethlehem, in Judaea, about five miles south of Jerusalem. He grew up plagued by his contemptuous elder brothers, and was employed by the family in the most menial and lowliest of tasks. His duty was to be herdsman to his father's flocks in the Judaean hills.

The story of how David was chosen to be king over Israel is told in the Bible. Here we read that God told Samuel to go to Jesse, the Bethlehemite 'for I have provided me a king among his sons'.[86] Samuel followed instructions, and one by one, the sons of Jesse passed before him, but God refused them.

'And Samuel said unto Jesse, Are here all thy children? And he said, There remaineth yet the youngest, and, behold, he keepeth the sheep. And Samuel said unto Jesse, Send and fetch him: for we will not sit down till he come hither.

'And he sent, and brought him in. Now he was ruddy, and withal of a beautiful countenance, and goodly to look to. And the Lord said, Arise, anoint him: for this is he.'[87]

So David received the spirit of the Lord, and found himself launched upon one of the stormiest careers in the history of his people.

The name of David has never been translated with any certainty. The nearest possibility upon which scholars can agree is 'beloved' but this interpretation has been questioned.

163

Now it has become certain that 'David' is not a name at all. Archaeologists digging through the ruins of an important city on the Euphrates, have unearthed tablets on which the word 'Davidum' appears again and again. Its meaning is 'commander' or 'general', and so we do not know what the real name of David was (any more than we know the name of Moses), although more is recorded of the details of his life and character than of almost any other figure in the Bible.

Solomon, the son of David, actually built the Temple in Jerusalem, but it was his father, David, who first planned it, and before he died had collected much of the material for it, in iron and wood and brass. The Old Testament gives us the story of how the idea came into being in the time of David.[88] It all started with a notion of David's to take a census! This proposed numbering of the people included the Benjamites. The Israelites in general, and particularly the Benjamites, were a very independent people, and they resented the idea of being counted. Almost a thousand years before the time of David, one of the governors of Mari wished to take just such a census of the desert tribes. One of his officers, Samsi-Addu, wrote to him in very strong terms, advising him to give up his plan. Dr Werner Keller quotes this letter from the eighteenth century BC.

'Reference the proposal to take a census of the Benjamites, about which you have written me. . . . The Benjamites are not well disposed to the idea of a census. If you carry it out, their kinsmen, the Ra-ab-ay-yi, who live on the other bank of the river, will hear of it. They will be annoyed with them and will not return to their country. On no account should this census be taken.'[89]

In the tenth century BC David ran headlong into the same problem. Joab, whom he put in charge of the operation, considered it a trespass, and he refused to count either the Benjamites or the Levites. They were displeased and so was their God. Gad, the Royal Seer, foresaw the punishment that would descend upon Israel for David's adoption of such an 'abominable' foreign practice. David was given a choice of three evils, and the story of how he subsequently bought and paid for a place upon which to build an altar to his God in

Jerusalem is related in the Old Testament. '. . . the tabernacle of the Lord, which Moses made in the wilderness, and the altar of the burnt offering, were at that season in the high place at Gibeon.'[90]

There follows a description of David's plans for the House of the Lord, which 'he had by the spirit', and many details of his preparations and of those of 'the chiefs of the fathers, and princes of the tribes of Israel',[91] are given. David knew from the beginning that he could not build the House, because he had shed too much blood. He was 'a man of blood', and therefore it was not fitting that he should actually erect the House of Peace. It was promised to him, however, that Solomon, his son, would build it, and because he did so it is called Solomon's Temple. Solomon usually gets all the credit, whereas it was a joint enterprise between David and Solomon, and although they were father and son, rather more than an echo appears of that duality usually associated with the two types of mankind called Brothers or Twins.

In this case, it was David who was the man of action, the soldier and patriot, concerned with the affairs of his people, and yet, in communication with Heaven (usually through his Seer), and Solomon, his son, was renowned for his wisdom. The latter's name is associated with the Hebrew Shelomon – 'his peace' – although, here again, some scholars are by no means certain of this rendering. The second member of the pair may be as anonymous as the first. Tradition points out that the form of his name we use today, and which we have through Greek usage and translation, Sol-om-on, is the name of the Sun in the language of the west, the east, and the Egyptian south.

Who were these men, really, who with the help of Heaven and its Angels, made Israel great? Certainly they were two most unusual Men. Why, then, were their true names concealed?

We shall probably never really know, at this late date, all the circumstances of the lives of David and Solomon which led to their impersonalisation, and then which led, again, to the near loss of all memory of it. It is another of the world's mysteries that scholarship may or may not be able, some day, to solve.

The fact remains, however, that King Solomon has had more associations of mystery, magic, and esoteric implication, hung about him than any other man who claimed to be an ordinary mortal. The days of the greatest glory of Israel as a nation were the days of Solomon. David, his father, had pushed the boundaries of control outward to face the advancing Assyrians, on the one hand, and the declining power of Egypt on the other. In Solomon's time, there was much trade with the full length of the Arabian peninsula, even to Yemen and the city of Marib, whence came the Queen of Sheba 'with camels that bare spices'. Archaeology has only recently uncovered more of his mining and copper-smelting operations in Arabia, complete with a type of blast-furnace rediscovered in the 1850s by an Englishman named Bessemer and applied in our own day to the manufacture of steel.

One place is so familiar its importance may have been overlooked. Solomon was on the best of terms with the Phoenicians. Tyre was a Phoenician city, and the contributions of Hiram, King of Tyre, are catalogued in the Bible, as well as the arrangements made between the two kings. We read, 'And there came of all people to hear the wisdom of Solomon, from all kings of the earth, which had heard of his wisdom.'[92] There may have been a few more of these visiting kings of whom modern thinking fails to take account, because it is the fashion in our time to think of the far West of Europe and the Mediterranean as sunk in the mists of barbarism, while the light shone only in the East. The Phoenicians had thought it profitable, however, to do business with Britain and Ireland, and for a very long time Egypt had been a good customer for Irish gold.

When Solomon raised the Temple of Jerusalem, it was with the willing help of many of these Phoenicians. Along with the skilled workmen in both wood and stone that King Hiram sent to King Solomon, there came a 'cunning man', another Hiram, Huram-Abi. In one Book in the Old Testament he is described as a worker in brass,[93] but another gives a much more interesting and detailed list of his talents.[94] Tradition credits him with taking over the general direction of the whole work. His mother was an Israelite. One story says she was of the tribe of Naphtali, another says Dan, but his father was a Phoenician. King Hiram's letter to Solomon says this Huram-Abi was 'skilful to work in gold, and in silver, in brass, in iron, in stone, and in timber, in purple, in blue, and in fine linen, and in crimson; also to grave any manner of graving and to find out every device which shall be put to him'.[95] He was truly a most versatile and all-round craftsman, as well as an architect who could have been trusted to follow and reproduce the inspired plans for the Temple which Solomon had inherited from his father.

As a Phoenician, Huram-Abi would have been acquainted with both the Egyptian style of building in hewn stone and with the megalithic architecture of the ancients. When he came to Jerusalem to build for Solomon, Stonehenge had been finished for 500 years. The worship of both the Phoenicians and the Israelites had much in common with that of the older, megalithic cultures, and the monuments of Britain were not insuperably far away as Phoenicians thought of travel.

An element of the ancient Age of Stone was incorporated in the Temple of Solomon. Neither the plans nor the description of the building mentions an altar for burnt-offering, very probably for the simple reason that an ancient, unhewn rock called the sakhra must have taken its place. This was a hallowed stone that had been venerated long before the days of King David. It was mentioned by Ezekiel and given a place of importance in his plans for a future temple, and in the seventh century, following the capture of Jerusalem, the Arabs built a beautiful structure over it called The Dome of the Rock, which still stands.

The connection of both Huram-Abi and King Solomon with building in stone was carried to England with the Craft of Freemasonry, and certain Degrees of this Craft have become the repository of much traditional lore connected with both great men. Masonic teachings regarding the nature of mankind, his esoteric history, and the ultimate destiny of Man have been woven about them, and about the building of Solomon's Temple, together with its rebuilding by Zerubbabel in the time of Haggai. With respect to all this, it is of the greatest importance to recall that England is and has always been looked upon as the home and headquarters of Masonry, once that organisation had developed, along with humanity, to a point where it could enter a cycle of outward manifestation in the world. The date chosen for the outward unification of the Lodges and the formation of the Mother Grand Lodge in England was St John's (The Baptist) Day, 1717. The time by the zodiac, was half a century before the true beginning of the new Aquarian Age.

The list of Masons who played important parts in setting the political, economic, philosophical, ethical, religious and scientific stage for the advent of an Aquarian world is both long and impressive. The practical, the hard-headed, and the down-to-earth may call enthusiasm to task for over-interpretation, but there are many who see in all this a restoration of that co-operative effort between the wise men and the workmen, between the architects and the builders and embellishers, that made possible in the days of Hiram and Solomon, the erection of a building which has remained for all time since a symbol of the creative ability and ultimate achievement of mankind. It should not be forgotten that the building of King Solomon's Temple was an international enterprise.

14.   A Century of Foundations

. . . the traditions of this building . . . are very reassuring.
                                                      —*The High Lama*

'The Renaissance if we try to regard it as a period, was essentially the transition from one historical age to another.'[96]

In the middle of the fifteenth century, after a thousand years of orthodoxy, the tide of European thinking began to turn away from the traditions of the old Empire and the Church. For a hundred years, Italy was the centre and fountainhead of this new burst of emotional and mental energy. By the middle of the sixteenth century, when other countries (notably England) had joined the forward surge, mankind was reaching out vigorously to make the whole world his and to better that world if he could. The medieval attitude that this earth was a vale of tears to be endured in hope of a better life to come was now obsolete. Mankind had begun to feel that he had a right to observe and to explore, and above all, to make use of his natural environment, and he was asserting that right, boldly and universally.

In this new expansion of consciousness, only China, oldest of all the kingdoms of the world, fell behind. When the Eastern Empire collapsed with the fall of Constantinople and the hope for a Western Empire of any significance deteriorated, along with the temporal power of the Papacy, the fire of the Renaissance was passed along to other and fresh torches. For the next hundred years after Italy released the great revival, England held the centre of the stage with Elizabeth, Shakespeare, Bacon and all the galaxy of figures in other fields, who spread the mind of European Man around the world.

Even the remote Orient felt the surge. In India, Akbar took his restricted heritage of a very small kingdom, and built it up to be the great Mogul Empire. His son, Jahangir and his wife, sustained the dreams of Akbar, and it was Jahangir's own son,

Shah Jahan, who built that incomparable masterpiece of architecture, the Taj Mahal.

At the same time in far-away Japan, the Hero Hideyoshi was unifying his country. Hideyoshi started life in a very humble way. He was groom to a certain Nobunaga, who had enlarged his domains by stubborn force over a period of a whole generation. In less time, through astute diplomacy and the exercise of much good common sense, Hideyoshi advanced himself, first to the place of regent, and finally, to the position of undisputed master of Japan 'from end to end'. Through his intelligent alliance with Tokugawa Tyeyasu, who survived him, Hideyoshi laid the foundations for a very great period in the history of the Japanese world. Before he died, Hideyoshi even dreamed of conquering China. It is an interesting problem for an evening's thought: What would our modern world have been like, today, had he succeeded? It may be of some significance that he began his campaign in Korea. At any rate, his dream did not come true. China is still China, and it alone of all the important nations of the world did not share in the Renaissance that took place, although it had been offered the elements by Marco Polo and his brothers, as early as the thirteenth century!

The sixth century BC and the sixteenth century AD occupy roughly the same positions in a zodiacal month, according to pyramid cycles. The period from about 600 BC to about 500 BC corresponds, in pattern, to the period between AD 1550 to AD 1650, plus or minus a few years. In the era of the zodiacal month of 2,152 years, it represents the next to the last day (and a little more) before the end . . . (of the month). If we compare the zodiacal month (age) with a lunar month, each day in the longer cycle will be found to be equal to about seventy-seven years – a very respected and Kabbalistic number.

Because of our present place in history it is impossible to compare in detail more than three of these cyclic beginnings, those of Aries, Pisces and our own age, Aquarius.

According to the cycles built into the Great Pyramid, the Age of Taurus ended, and the Age of Aries began about 2500 BC. If we look at the civilisations our archaeologists have given back to us about that time, we will see a definitely similar condition of affairs to the two we have been considering. About 2700 BC the kings of Egypt entered into a period of greatness and prosperity, where it became possible for them to attempt to copy the Great Pyramid in the erection of their own tombs. One of them, according to some thoughts on the subject, was even crass enough to enter the secret chambers of that mighty edifice and leave his signature, much as people today leave their names written on the railings of bridges and in other important places. 'Cheops was here'. It is a very natural and omnipresent manifestation of humanity. Cheops, in this field, certainly takes precedence over the Kilroy of this civilisation's Second World War.

The beginnings of the Age of Taurus lie far back, well beyond Bishop Usher's date for the 'creation of Adam', which marks for us the traditional beginning of our own history. The revisers of the zodiac orientated their computations to the year 4699 BC. Since this is before 'the beginning', it is certain that they worked their calculations backward to include the time of upheaval and to come out even with the position of the stars. This is no great mathematical miracle, and agrees well with the workings of human psychology. They bridged the gap caused by the geological catastrophes which took place about 4000 BC, and they built well.

If there was a comparable period of learning and a similar forward surge of endeavour toward the end of the Taurean Age, it was obliterated by the natural disasters accompanying the end of that era. According to our presumed (and admittedly presumptuous) pattern, it would have taken place about 4900 and 4800 BC.

We must be content, therefore, with our three examples, within the accepted limits of our discussion – the pyramid datings of zodiacal months or ages.

Hardly ever in the history of the world has there been a century so full of promise or so active with the progress of human thought, as the sixth century before the advent of Jesus of Nazareth. The world is still trying to live up to the ideals of at least ten of the Men who were prominent in that one hundred years. And there were others. Space does not permit a full catalogue of all the important figures who arose and who played their part in this beginning of the end – for

171

such it was. Not only were they taking part in the culmination of a single zodiacal month, but they were laying the groundwork for an entire new Astrological Year. Aries was their next age, and it was both the first and the last. The Cycle of Precession takes the world backward through the list of signs. Pisces, the following sign, marked the beginning of a new age of not only 2,152 years, but of a major cycle of more than 25,000 years. Preparations for such a change were not only very important, they could be expected to have very far-reaching consequences, and this has proved to be true. We are still trying to follow the sign posts set up by the Men who lived and attempted to teach other men between 600 and 500 BC. That we have not been able to do so, is no reflection upon either our zeal or our understanding. After all, we are only a little way into the next zodiacal year – somewhere about the beginning of February, in fact. Their prophetic comprehension included the whole cycle, which will not end for many thousands of years to come. We must not judge mankind too harshly, then, if we look at his affairs in this light.

Who were these Men who set up the patterns we are still trying to follow and to complete in our own time? Who gave us that set of values the later prophets and teachers, moreover, have only been able to elaborate and to develop, and which we still find difficult to follow out to the letter of the law? Who were these geniuses who came along at the end of a Great Precessional Year and set the tone for the next cycle? They were a most remarkable company of Men.

The first among them was a Greek called Thales who was born about 640 BC. He has been called the Chief of the Seven Wise Men of Greece. He was a politician, a merchant, a mathematician, a philosopher and an astronomer. One of his astronomical calculations has caused no end of controversy in learned circles. He is said to have predicted an eclipse of the Sun for 28 May, 585 BC. which interrupted and ended a battle between the Medes and the Lydians. This led to a final reconciliation between the two countries. The argument goes that he could not have done this according to the accepted mathematics of his time. What that argument leaves out is the question: was Thales restricted to the accepted mathematics of his time? Apparently, he was not otherwise confined. He introduced linear geometry and produced equations from which Algebra was developed – much later. He postulated that the angular diameter of the Sun is 1/720th part of the full circle of the zodiac. And he corrected the year. By his time the old Babylonian year of 360 days had become inaccurate. He brought the calculations up to date, by his observations. 'Not in name only, but also in fact, Thales, the first of the Ionian Physicists, was the founder of the philosophy of Greece.'[97]

From the time of Thales great names began to fall, literally, out of the sky. They are names to conjure with. Solon; Ezekiel; Jeremiah; Li Urh who was called Lao Tze ('The Old Boy'); Siddartha Gautama, Buddha; Cyrus the Great, Croesus, the merchant king of Lydia; Confucius; and Ezra, the scribe and priest who, at the time of the return of the Hebrew people to Jerusalem under Nehemiah, founded the Great Synagogue, restored the law, and rewrote the sacred records, which had been destroyed. This list does not even include Darius, who founded the Persian Empire, or Haggai, who badgered Zerubbabel into laying the foundations for the second Temple at Jerusalem.

It was a century of genius – such genius as the world has yet to live up to, since it initiated not only the end of a zodiacal month, but the termination and beginning of an entire zodiacal year – more than 25,000 circuits of the planet Earth around its sun. We are still only beginning to work out the pattern of life and understanding laid down by these Men, who lived and tried to reach the world, two and a half millennia ago. Like King Solomon, we have inherited the plans and architectural design for a mighty temple, the temple of Mankind. Like Solomon when he wrote to Hiram, King of Tyre, to enlist his aid in carrying out the designs of David, we are looking for help and co-operation.

All the thousands of years since 'the beginning', as our traditional history records it, have piled up not only the blueprints but much of the material for our projected edifice. We have already begun to build. We may feel that some of our building has gone awry, and we may even feel that part of the structure may collapse, due to our own bungling.

But, are we alone? Do we work alone?

Assuredly, we do not. *Mankind on earth has never worked alone*. He has always had all the guidance he is able to accept, as such. Advice will never come his way in any other form. If mankind goes out into the galaxy it will be as Man, independent and individual. Nobody out there has time to take him by the hand and lead him about as a helpless infant, or under-age tourist. If he goes, then it will be with the key to the front door in his hand, or not at all.

Within the period of his recorded history, mankind on earth has accumulated all he needs to know about himself and his environment. The Age of Aquarius, into which he has already entered without really being aware of the fact, is pre-eminently the age of analysis and synthesis. Its energies and impulses will enable him to look at what he has accumulated, see it for what it is, and put it together into a new and very practical pattern which will work . . . for the next 25,000 years.

When the new pattern takes shape it may not look very much like the old one his historical traditions have taught him to respect. On the contrary, it may be a very different kind of pattern, indeed. However, by the time he begins to see what it is and where it is going, it will become beautiful in his eyes. It will be worthy of his very best efforts, and mankind will be able to dedicate himself, with all the one-pointed energy of the great cycle of Capricorn, to its ultimate fulfilment, and his own.

15. The Price of Unity

This fellow must have been mad from the beginning. . . .
Very well organised lunacy, you know. – *Mallinson and Conway*

The man-god who was to become King of Macedonia, Pharaoh of Egypt, Hegemon of the Greeks, King of Babylonia, Persia and Media, conqueror of Asia, and who was to extend his empire to the very foot of the Himalayas, was born in 356 BC. He is known to history as Alexander the Great. His father was Philip, who at Alexander's birth was Regent of Macedonia, and his mother, one of the sacred Hetairae of the Temple, a princess of Epirus, called Olympias.

There were many strange facets attached to Alexander's birth. Although Philip was called his father, many tales have come down to us that the future conqueror of the known world was conceived as the result of a union between Olympias and the god Zeus-Ammon in the guise of a snake. In those far-off times it was the custom for girls of high birth to take part in the Temple ceremonies and to become initiated into the Mysteries. In many of these temples snakes were accorded symbolic reverence.

Some writers have stated that the virgin temple girl, Olympias, was with child when Philip married her, and he is reported to have been very disturbed upon discovering the state of affairs. However, the birth of a great prince – a veritable god-king – had been foretold by the wise man and the astrologers of the period. It could very possibly have been arranged by the High Priest of the Temple and other Initiates for Olympias (who had become an Initiate) to be matched with a specially selected individual possessing exceptional physique, heritable gifts, and unusual ability. At any rate, tradition has it that the priests of Ephesus prophesied the coming of Alexander with these words: 'This day there is in some part of the world a torch kindled which shall one day consume all the Orient.' It is also told that on the night that the future king was born there was a violent thunderstorm with much lightning, which was taken as a sign from Zeus himself, and two black eagles are said to have been observed sitting on the roof of the palace. This was taken to mean that the new prince would one day rule over two empires. Certainly, the omens were later to be borne out in no uncertain manner.

In future years Alexander came to be regarded in Persia, Babylonia and Egypt, as being of divine birth, and there is no doubt that during his short life span he accomplished more than any ordinary mortal could have done in a thousand years. I do not propose to go into details of his campaigns here. They are on record for those who are interested. He crossed the Hellespont. He conquered the Troad. He captured Damascus, which led to the conquest of Syria and Phoenicia. He was crowned Pharaoh of Egypt at Memphis. He took Babylon and Persia. The whole of the Orient was his. Afghanistan, Baluchistan, Turkestan and Samarkand, all fell to Alexander's triumphant army. There has never been another comparable military genius. Some talk of Hannibal and some of Napoleon, but Alexander has never been equalled in the field of military achievement.

In Eastern Phrygia there was a place called Gordium. The legend has come down to us that a peasant called Gordius had tied a raw-hide knot on an ox-yoke. An eagle perched on it, and this was taken as a sign that the gods had chosen Gordius for a royal destiny. He eventually married a priestess and became King of Phrygia. Afterwards he built a great fortress at what came to be called Gordium and the yoke was preserved there. Gordius dedicated the yoke to Zeus himself.

Gordium became a key position in that it controlled and lay across the main route through Asia. In short, you had to take Gordium if your desire was to rule the Orient. Local tradition said that whoever untied the Gordian Knot would become the ruler of the whole of Asia. Alexander began at Gordium the campaign that ended in the defeat of Darius at Issus. Therefore, it can be said that he cut the Gordian Knot with a sword.

At a higher level of interpretation the Gordian Knot symbolises the complicated problems of mankind. The sword, wherever it appears in symbolism, be it as Arthur's Excalibur, Michael's Sword, or, in this case, the sword of Alexander, is the symbol of Creative Mind in contrast to the merely analytical and synthetic functions. The solution of mankind's problems can be found only through the application of creative mental energy, which has the effect of destroying the problems at once and for ever.

The story is told that Alexander wished to visit the Oracle of Jupiter Ammon. This was situated in an oasis in the centre of the Libyan Desert. To reach this spot Alexander set out on the long journey across the sandy wilderness, accompanied by a large escort of his troops – in fact, a small army. Suddenly a strong wind came up, which caused the sand to rise and erase all signs of the track the army was following. Those who were guiding the king did not know which way to pursue, and the army was completely lost. They could easily have perished of thirst and starvation in the sandy wastes.

One of Alexander's greatest generals, Ptolemy, who subsequently wrote a history of his campaigns, describes how two dragons suddenly appeared at the head of the army, making articulate sounds. Alexander gave the order to follow them, and they led the way straight to the Oracle. It will be recalled that in another earlier chapter we discussed the Druids and how in their time they were referred to as 'Ravens', 'Eagles', 'Finches', 'Swallows', and so forth. The serpent has always been the symbol of wisdom, and from time immemorial has been regarded as both a royal and a celestial symbol. It is only since the coming of Christianity that the serpent has been regarded as evil as a result of the misinterpretation of the Garden of Eden story. This I have discussed elsewhere, and I then also remarked that the serpent 'is a representation of the two major arms of the spiral galaxy in which we live, and is, therefore, the symbol of Galactic civilisation as well as the sigil of the Great Creator'.[98]

The serpent, then, is very much connected with the Sky and with Sky People. So, if we hear of 'serpents' or 'dragons' meeting and talking to Alexander in a time of desperate difficulty and bringing him and his army safely to their destination, it could quite conceivably have been Sky People who put in an appearance at that critical moment. The gods, they say, always watch over their own.

Many people, after crediting Alexander with prowess as a military genius, nevertheless regarded him as a dissolute, cruel and megalomaniac character. It is true, he drank his full quota of wine, but in those days that was expected.

Alexander was a person who was different from the rest of humanity. Imagine someone today, living here on this planet, whose knowledge and thought was thousands of years ahead of his fellow beings. He would, for a start, be a very lonely man. He would be unable to talk – really talk – on equal terms with anyone. That, of course, is what happened to Jesus, a little over 300 years later. True, the Nazarene chose a few other Men to be his disciples – his co-workers and colleagues, but even so he remained far ahead of them. He, too, was the loneliest of men. This is what always happens when someone from Out There incarnates in this chemical world. He is different. He cannot communicate at his own level.

Alexander was, of course, although we think descended from the gods, also a human being. He was a half-breed god, and therefore subject, like Jesus, to human difficulties. They were born within a few centuries of one another, and each had a different task to undertake.

Alexander's job was to finish off an old pattern. He was a man of action in a position to unite the many small city states into one empire. The work of Jesus was essentially in the philosophic field. He had to try to establish a basis of understanding within the framework of which co-operation on a large scale among different peoples would be possible. His work was a long-term project for a new age, and it required time to develop and come to fruition. It should be remembered that although he was descended from the Royal Line of David, in his particular day and age he was not in the same position as Alexander, and was not immediately concerned with ruling the kingdoms of this world. His functions were more abstract, even though his contemporaries expected him to take over the temporal kingdom of the Jews in a very literal sense.

Alexander knew who he was. He realised that he had

superior abilities and a greater mind than others. What happens to the superior schoolboy today, who in a lesser degree has more talents than his fellows? He is often goaded and taunted by the other boys. Alexander's friends, even in later life, behaved in the same way. There is, as an example of this, the well-known incident where he was jibed at during a feast by his best friend, Cleitus – an incident which ended in tragedy.

Of course Alexander was human. He knew that, but as must happen in such cases as his, the accusation was only half true. Those attacking him could not know and were not capable of understanding the whole truth. Consciously or unconsciously, many people resent superiority in others because they feel threatened by it. They cannot imagine anyone using such magnified abilities for any other purpose than increasing personal power and self-importance. Unless the man of ability gives them constant reassurance by behaving at all times in a meek, humble and most apparently harmless manner, they will fear him, and they will attack.

It could be questioned that Alexander the Great was a legitimate meddler in the affairs of the world because he was responsible for so much war and conquest, and for the killing of so many people, but such a question could only come out of another time than the one in which Alexander lived and with which he had to cope. In the first place, Alexander, whoever his real father may have been, was not dropped out of a space ship. He incarnated himself as a human being and attempted to accomplish what he set out to do in human ways – the human ways of his time and place – and by the human standards current in those times and throughout the world he unified.

In order to communicate with anybody very well we must speak his language, and Alexander spoke the language of military action according to the usage of his time. His world was divided into unbelievably small and generally uncommunicative kingdoms, many of them not much bigger than the village areas of our own day. Out of these conflicting and continually fighting political segments, Alexander set out in the footsteps of his father, Philip, who had begun the job as a sort of precursor, and proceeded to create the foundations of what we now know as the civilised world.

It is difficult to judge, fairly, the actions of people who lived in remote times, thousands of years ago, because we tend to apply standards and acceptances appropriate to our own more advanced understanding. These standards, although inevitably more moral, and more ethical perhaps, than those of our remote ancestors, might not have been applicable in those far-away times for the simple reason that nobody had invented them or realised them yet, with the possible exception of a very few philosophers who were certainly not in full control of the destiny of nations.

Alexander was in a better position to control these nations, as the king and the son of a line of kings. He could act. The philosophers could only talk, and it is really only those people in a position to act in this world who can tear down the old circumstances and set up new directions of activity more in line with the theories of the philosophers.

It was Alexander's privilege to study with at least one of the great philosophers – Aristotle – whose ideas have formed the basis for western thought up to the present. What he did, however deplorable it may appear to us from our more enlightened point of view and against our own background of very different circumstances, with thousands of years of political, moral and social evolution on our side, accomplished the birth of whatever civilisation we now possess. Birth is always painful, and it is never entirely beautiful.

16. Mankind Accepts His World

People make mistakes in life through believing too much, but they have a damned dull time if they believe too little.

— *Rutherford*

How far can we depend upon a legend or a myth to contain fact? Just as far we would say, as we can depend upon words and the structure of the ideas they present, to reflect the content of the mind or minds that formed and preserved them.

In spite of what many people would like to believe, mankind is not a very inventive creature. Given a good idea, he can, in the space of a few hundred or a few thousand years, elaborate upon it and refine its applications. The organisation of totally new ideas is, however, 'a sometimes and a seldom thing' in the history of Man. It occurs only now and again, as if by some long and cyclic revival of the impulse to think, the urge to perceive and to deal with facts, the impetus and the desire to be aware of himself in relationship to his environment.

All too soon, such a cycle of renaissance degenerates to the level of dramatisation. Then we see again the age of story-telling, the age of evasion and irresponsibility, the time of the dressed up idea and the diluted truth. Perhaps such a period could be called the Age of Entertainment.

It is an era that follows a time of glut and surfeit, of enjoyment without much further improvement of some occasionally produced invention or new process. Like the Stone Age it is a period in the development and applications of an idea, rather than any definite, datable period of time, and the Age of Entertainment for one idea may coincide with the Age of Invention for another.

In the long run, however, this does not appear to happen except in isolated and exceptional instances. If we look at history as a whole, we see the form of the process repeating itself through cycle after cycle, and it may be of some comfort and encouragement to astrologers that, for some reason – be it only coincidence – these cycles coincide closely with the motions of the zodiac. We say this with no intention to uphold, protect or advocate the vagaries of haphazard astrology. It is simply stated as another naked and unashamed (and, perhaps, uncomfortable) fact. If we can discover what that fact means, perhaps we may release the further disclosure of some principle that has kept astrology alive throughout thousands of years of shabby misrepresentation and misuse.

People do not expend centuries of effort upon the practice and preservation of totally useless notions. Man is an intensely practical creature, even when he sets out to achieve his own destruction, and a majority of mankind has always maintained that an understanding of the stars is some sort of signpost pointing the other way, toward a better and fuller understanding of Life and Purpose in the Universe.

If we can lay aside for the moment all the accumulated mass of elaborately detailed and personal interpretation, and look, quite simply and straightforwardly at the whole sweep of human history, we may observe a fact. We may not be able to say at once exactly what that fact means or why it exists, but we can say: There it is! Let's acknowledge its existence and take a good look at it. Maybe, we can find some use for it.

Astrology is a very old subject. It began as a science. It has passed through all the known stages in the life of an idea, and today the successful astrologer in the world (successful in terms of accuracy and application, rather than in terms of followings or bank accounts) is treating the study of the stars as a science. Orthodox, material scientists, of course, will have no official connection with such an antiquated, primitive idea. Science in any age is always 'modern'. It must be 'new'. The age of science coincides with the age of adolescence in any cycle. It is a product of the period of going ahead without regard for the past, without dependence upon the advice or knowledge of the Elders. It is one-pointed, concentrating upon the discovery of useful absolutes, and contemptuous of any previously presented 'facts', not clearly and immediately connected with its own acceptances.

Because of this attitude, in any scientific period, much that has been discovered in the past is rejected and thrown aside as irrelevant superstition. Then, inevitably, the time arrives when the pattern of acceptance demands the revival and recognition of some old legendary piece of knowledge that has been staring up out of the scrap-heap. Wonderingly, and often almost surreptitiously, it is resurrected and placed again in the Hall of Science like the marble head of some decapitated Apollo. The professors marvel at the fortunate guess that led the ancestors to such a close approximation of Modern Theory.

Astrology is not new, and something of the sort may yet happen to it in our own age of science, if we will but consent to examine its fundamentals. Operators of short-wave radio systems learned years ago that those positions of the major planets known as squares and conjunctions can put their broadcasting stations into serious difficulties and with a bit of additional help from an over-active Sun can disrupt communications altogether. One wonders which is the more sensitive – *a short-wave radio set, or the human brain*?

Both astrology and astronomy tell us that a zodiacal age lasts about 2,152 years, and represents approximately one-twelfth of a complete major cycle of 25,824 years. A new major cycle began about 395 BC, when the Sun entered the First Zodiacal Month – the twelfth – of the zodiac, the Sign of Pisces. The 'New Age' being given so much publicity these days is the second period of this major cycle of about 25,000 years, and its heralds numbered among them, Jesus, who was called The Christ. So, in order to understand 'New Age' prophecy and revelation at all well, it is first absolutely necessary to know what we are talking about when we use the term. We ought not to confine ourselves to too little time. The minutes of a day ought not to be confused with the hours, however legitimate both designations may be.

The grand New Age in which the biblical peoples were interested – because its beginning concerned them directly, lying as it did close to their times – is the whole, entire and complete Great Cycle of the Precession of the Equinoxes. The cycle incorporating within itself all the lesser of the twelve zodiacal signs – about 25,000 years.

The 'New Age' with which most contemporary 'prophets' concern themselves is the era of the Sign of Aquarius which – counting backwards as we must do because the Sun seems to move in that direction – is the second era in the new cycle, and lasts about 2,152 years.

Now, according to the system of pyramid dating discussed earlier, we are *not awaiting* the beginning of the Age of Aquarius. On the contrary, we are already well and truly in it. According to calculations based upon the pyramid, we *entered the Sign of Aquarius at about* AD *1750*, plus or minus a few years.

Jesus was symbolised as a lamb, because although the Age of Aries (the Ram) had ended before his birth, the effects of the age were still continuing, still mingling with incoming characteristics of the New Age of Pisces, whose symbol of a fish is also very much associated with the Nazarene. He was thought of as the lamb who was slain, but in his resurrection was symbolised as the fish, and he promised his disciples that they should be fishers of men!

It is interesting to note that the cross was not adopted as a symbol of Christianity until long after the death of Jesus. The symbol previously most used was the fish – the Sign of the Age of Pisces – the first era in the Grand Cycle of the Precession. Christians used the sign of the fish as a secret sign for a long time before the cross came into general usage. Actually, the cross is far from being exclusively a Christian sign. It had been used in the *Crux Ansanta*, in Ancient Egypt; as the *Tau* in China; and it had also been used by the Chaldeans, the Phoenicians, the Peruvians and the Mexicans, among others. It is one of the most ancient of all the symbols in the world, and its oldest counterpart is the swastika, which has been found in antediluvian rock carvings on every continent.

The Sign of Aquarius (the Water-Bearer or Cup-Bearer) is then, the one we are now in, and it began about AD 1750. It is the Age of the Analytical Mind – the era of specialised knowledge. From its inception onwards discoveries began to pour in upon us. The planet Uranus was discovered in 1781. The steam-engine in 1825. The aeroplane at the beginning of our own century. Now we read almost daily of new developments in Electronics, Nuclear Fission and other specialised fields. More than at any other time in the last 10,000 years this is the Age of Specialisation. Technological knowledge is progressing so fast that a man employed in one scientific sphere has his 'work cut out' for him to keep up with all the new applications and the continued necessary study of his own subject, let alone to cope with another, except in a very general way.

True, there are, of course, still exceptional people to be found in the world who can be called 'all round men', but they are prominent in the realms of politics, literature and the arts, rather than in the ever-advancing fields. In the Piscean Age, on the other hand, it was possible for an exceptional man to have all-round knowledge in both the arts and in science, within the limited thinking of those days. It was dangerous to communicate your thoughts too much, openly, especially if they did not conform with the prevalent view. Original ideas were usually regarded as heresy or witchcraft by the Church.

Before a new age begins, it can be affirmed with some justification that 'coming events cast their shadows before them'. Planetary influences may well start to be gradually felt some centuries previous to their actual culmination. The Moon, as is well known, affects the ocean tides, but its influences on the waters have been at work for many hours before Full Tide is reached.

A man who can be said to have definitely paved the way for the Aquarian Age, and to have found the means – at some considerable risk to himself – of breaking through the dogmatic thought of his time, was born in 1452. The birth of Leonardo da Vinci occurred about 300 years before the Aquarian Age began. His mother was a barmaid at an inn. His father was thought to be a certain Signor who took an interest in him and his mother, but she would not confirm this assumption, which was odd, since there was nothing particularly unusual or indecent about being a recognised illegitimate in that day and time.

In early history, those whose fathers were of royal blood suffered no stigma from being born out of wedlock. 'Among the Franks we find Theodoric I, a natural son of Clovis, sharing the kingdom with the legitimate sons: Zwentibold, natural son of Arnulf, was created king of Lorraine by his father in 805; and even William the Conqueror actually assumed the appellation of bastard.'[99]

It is, too, quite astonishing to catalogue the number of outstanding men who have influenced the course of history and shaped the destinies of their fellows, whose parentage has been obscure.

In prehistory, there is the example of the original King Arthur. Since recorded history began we can mention Moses, who was found in the bullrushes by an Egyptian princess. Sargon, too, was similarly discovered in a basketful of rushes by Akki. Philip of Macedonia was doubtful about the parentage of his son, Alexander the Great, and, Joseph was concerned soon after he married the Temple Virgin, Mary, for he found that she was already with child.

Leonardo da Vinci was one of the most complete men in every mental department, not only of his day and age, but of any time. He had absolute self-assurance – the same inborn confidence of 'knowing' – that Nikola Tesla had in his own more specialised era, and both men were ahead of their time.

Leonardo was one of the world's greatest painters. His Virgin of the Rocks (the original is in the Louvre); the fabulous Last-Supper; the Virgin and St Anne; the world-famous La Gioconda (the Mona Lisa, also in the Louvre); these pictures have all helped to make his name immortal in that one artistic sphere alone. But he was capable of turning his hand to anything, and he was a consummate artist at whatever work he undertook. We have on record his magnificent, sculptured equestrian Sforza monument.

Leonardo's employers included Ludovico Sforza, Duke Cesare Borgia, and Francis I, King of France. He excelled as a masque and pageant master, whenever his patrons called upon him to organise their elaborate and costly fêtes. However, it was not only as a pageant master that he was employed by these powerful and influential men, but as an architect and as an engineer, in both military and civil capacities.

The many-sided Leonardo was, in fact, brilliant in many fields, besides those of the arts. He was no mean mathematician, and was engaged in both physical and anatomical research. His wonderful anatomical drawings were exhibited in London a few years ago. He was also a writer and a philosopher. He made copious notes which were always intended by him for the use of humanity, but owing to the circumstances of his life he was never able to complete the task of co-ordinating them for the purpose of publication.

Leonardo can be compared with the celebrated Count St Germain. Both had an almost supernatural – or, so it might seem to many people – knowledge *par excellence* of so many facets of life. Leonardo and the Count were both skilled in music. Both were brilliant in the sciences and the arts. Both were athletic. Leonardo was an expert horseman.

Although Leonardo had his friends – he was on good terms with many leading scientists of the day, such as Paolo Toscanelli, the well-known astronomer, and with Benedetto Aritmetico, the physician – he shut himself up for long periods, both for work and for meditation. He was, of course, in many ways a very lonely man, as anyone so different and so knowledgeable as Leonardo, must inevitably be. If you are odd, different, and your attainments make you seem superior, this is often resented by those in your immediate vicinity. This is what happened to Leonardo in his youth. Furthermore, in later life his rivals, chiefly Michelangelo, sensed the natural superiority of Leonardo and openly showed rank jealousy. This resentment is shown to anyone who proves himself more capable than his fellows – who does not conform – it is one of the characteristics of the human race.

Leonardo was contemporary with both Raphael and Michelangelo. The latter was a superb craftsman and a master sculptor, but he was a moody, bitter man, who had suffered much in his rise to the top of his profession and taunted his rivals, whenever the opportunity arose.

Leonardo knew what he was capable of, and did not find it necessary to enter into these arguments. He was not a hostile person by nature. No doubt, like the Nazarene, he could be angry if it was necessary. Leonardo was always courteous and noble in his bearing when dealing with others. Although he painted a magnificent battle scene, Leonardo abhorred war which he described as a 'bestial frenzy'.[100]

He was not for or against the teachings of the Church. He lived in an age when the Roman Catholic Church was supreme and his patrons were closely connected with it. Duke Cesare Borgia was the son of Pope Alexander VI, and was created a cardinal himself. It was an era of dogma and superstition. A dangerous time for Leonardo to have lived in, and indeed, his pioneer researches and experiments in natural science inevitably brought charges against him of working with the Devil. He was accused of being a magician and of heresy. Fortunately, however, he managed to clear himself.

Nevertheless, Leonardo had to adopt the practice of writing his notes from right to left, and also, upside down. They could only be read by the use of a mirror. This precaution kept his work from being read by prying curious eyes who would not understand. Leonardo too, living as we have said, in an age before his time, had to be careful as to what he offered mankind.

To some extent Leonardo can be compared with Tesla. Both men in their respective periods were regarded by those who were close to them with something like awe. Like Tesla, Leonardo did not marry, but dedicated his whole life to creative work and research. Tesla did not achieve the universal and lasting fame of Leonardo, partly as the result of living in a more specialised age. Nevertheless, he devoted his whole life to offering a more advanced technology to humanity. Both were looked upon as beings who were different from the ordinary stream of humanity. Indeed, Francis I, who was Leonardo's patron in the last years of his life, declared his 'knowledge of the fine arts and philosophy to be beyond those of all mortal men'.

The Master died on 2 May, 1519. He was truly a Man – a giant among mankind.

About fourteen years later in England, a princess of the Royal House of Tudor, was born at Greenwich Palace on Sunday, 7 September, 1533. The daughter of Henry VIII and the ill-fated Anne Boleyn, from the very earliest age Elizabeth showed signs of remarkable intellect. She had a very unhappy childhood. Her mother was beheaded and her father arranged to have not only his marriage with Anne Boleyn dissolved, but his daughter excluded from the succession. The executions of both her mother and, later, of her step-mother, Catherine Howard, affected her intensely. These occurrences caused her to form a justifiable prejudice against marriage.

Elizabeth received an excellent education from such tutors as Roger Ascham and Baldassare Castiglione. She was an apt, ready and industrious pupil. This capacity for work was to continue throughout her life. Like Alexander, who sat up all night planning and working out details of his campaign for the next day's batttle, while his men slept in their tents; like da Vinci and Tesla who both worked through the long night hours at their tasks, so it is on record that Elizabeth when she took over the affairs of state as queen, devoted herself to many hours of concentrated work at a stretch, without sleep. Ascham stated that her mind was more like a man's. He had never seen a more retentive memory. She became skilled in both Greek and Latin, besides four modern languages. Her handwriting was exquisite and beautifully clear. In other subjects she was equally versed. Elizabeth even learned the language of her Welsh ancestor, Owen Tudor, a descendant of the last of The Arthurs, Caradoc.

The future queen's youth was filled with jeopardy, brought about by changing political intrigues and plots. However, partly through her own inborn skill she managed to literally keep her head not only above water, but away from the block.

On 17 November, 1558, both Mary Tudor and her cousin, Cardinal Pole, died within a few hours of each other, and Elizabeth became Queen of England.

Her accession was greeted with great rejoicing by the people. The new queen was essentially English and immensely popular with her subjects. She knew how to please them and was constantly moving among them with very little body-guard. A sharp contrast to other European countries usually immersed in civil war or strife. Foreign ambassadors were frequently amazed by the ease with which her coach moved among the crowds with little protection.

Elizabeth had a talent for saving money, and very seldom asked her people for any. This further endeared the queen to her subjects. No doubt this helped when the time came for her to ask the Lord Mayor of London for men and ships when the Spanish Armada was threatening the soil of England. The people gladly provided twice the number of men and ships requested.

There was only one major point on which her ministers disagreed with the queen, and that was the question of marriage. They saw only too clearly that if she did not marry, the country might become the prey of both a foreign and Roman Catholic ruler. However, on this point the queen was adamant. She played most successfully for time, and encouraged the suits of foreign princes and flirted with her own handsome courtiers, including Ralegh, Leicester and Essex.

The 17th November, 1558, the day on which the Elizabethan reign or era began – the date of decision – is a Pyramid date for the 'cycle of higher induction'. It is, also, as already mentioned, the date of the deaths of both Mary Tudor and Cardinal Pole. It is, also, the day remembered in Egypt as the date on which is commemorated the death of Osiris.

What was the task to which Elizabeth and certain groups of people devoted themselves in those times? Briefly, these were to stabilise western civilisation in this world. To synthesise its already existing components. In short, to further the Renaissance, so well begun in the arts and the sciences by Leonardo and his contemporaries. Furthermore, to extend this work, take it over and to expand it outward into the world.

Because of the archaic features incorporated into the Roman Catholic Church, it was not desirable to allow all of western thought and culture to fall into the hands of Rome. Hence, the broader and more liberal form of Protestantism was established in England, at the capstone of the chief magnetic centre for the world, from whence it spread.

What events occurred in Elizabethan England towards attaining this end?

On the non-material level: There were the men – Bacon, Dyer, Shakespeare, and probably four others – who wrote the Shakespearean plays, which are prophetic, as well as pertinent to their own times (a neglected aspect). There were the beginnings of true scientific thought and research; the commencement of enlightened political policy; and, the birth of modern social consciousness.

On the material level: Improvements in technology, including naval design; the development of modern naval organisation; geographical expansion (witness Drake, Ralegh, Hawkins, Frobisher, Gilbert and others), and the initial establishment of the British Empire (Virginia and Newfoundland), as a necessary step in the civilisation of the western hemisphere on the one hand, and the formation of a strong bond with the eastern hemisphere on the other.

On the whole: The formation and establishment of the matrix from which a unified western culture pattern could emerge in all possible freedom, and within which the individual became of paramount importance as an active, more or less self-determining formative-creative factor in the development of society. None of this had been possible since the misdirection of the original Christian ideal.

It is interesting to compare the tasks of that Elizabethan period with the present one. One of the jobs now, in contemporary Elizabethan times is the further extension and expansion of mankind's conscious awareness into Outer Space – the space of this chemical universe.

The first Elizabeth, through her brilliant statecraft and adroitness in diplomacy, was able to stave off the attempted invasion of Britain by Catholic Spain until 1588. In the meantime, she had encouraged and inspired the exploits of her seamen – many of these had been rank piracy – and, when at last the Spanish Armada set sail under the command of the Duke of Medina-Sidonia, they received a sound drubbing from Lord Howard of Effingham's fleet, whose ships were captained by such experienced seadogs as Drake and Frobisher.

Elizabeth's work, then, was to keep England out of war as long as possible and be ready to deal with the Spaniards if the need arose. This she accomplished and her seamen did the rest. However, the defeat of the Armada and the inevitable loss of the mastery of the seas by Spain, was not the only outcome of her work. Elizabeth had, as a result, thwarted Rome. The Renaissance was now assured. The pioneer work of Leonardo, Shakespeare and Bacon, could go on, and be continued by others. Individuals would still be able to think freely along their own self-chosen lines. Elizabeth's policies of encouraging thought in different directions to those fostered by the Church of Rome could develop in even more security. This British way of life and culture would not now be erased, as the Romans had successfully removed all traces of the Ancient Britons' culture over half a millennium before.

Elizabeth, although she never married, was in her own time almost a legendary figure. The Pope said at the time of the Armada, 'She is a great woman; and were she only Catholic she would be without her match.'[101]

There has been no one quite like this paradoxically brilliant queen. Brave and fearful, pacifist and patriot, generous and parsimonious, kind and cruel – but, above all, a lover of and a believer in England, and its future destiny. She was probably the greatest queen and, indeed ruler, that England has ever had in recorded historical times.

Do you recall her famous great speech at Tilbury, with the Spanish Armada even then on its way up the English Channel? '. . . I know that I have the body of a weak and feeble woman, but I have the heart and stomach of a king, and of a King of England, too; and I think foul scorn that Parma, or Spain, or any prince of Europe should dare to invade the borders of my realm; to which rather than any dishonour should grow by me, I will myself take up arms, I myself will be your general, judge and rewarder of every one of your virtues in the field.'

By her skill, leadership and achievements, this remarkable woman saved and perpetuated both England and the Renaissance, and thus helped to prepare for the incoming New Age. She, too, was a Man among mankind.

17. New Times, New Teaching

. . . entire philosophies were unfolded; the long avenues of history surrendered themselves for inspection and were given new plausibility. — Lost Horizon

It is a matter for some reflection that Benjamin Franklin, rightly regarded as one of America's greatest diplomatists, is not properly given his rightful place in history as having been the leading individual who influenced and inspired not only the successful conclusion of the American War of Independence (for his own country and, perhaps, the world) but the French Revolution.

If we investigate the many-sided activities of this remarkable man and take a deeper look into the nature of Franklin himself, a lot more is to be seen than is apparent on the surface. Let us dive overboard then and see what we can bring up. Our first find is that he was both a Rosicrucian and a Freemason. Furthermore, we discover that he was a Quaker. An interesting combination.

It seems that we have to keep diving down into the waters again and again, for there is so much of value to be found. The list of Franklin's occupations is endless – diplomat, statesman, scientist, writer, philosopher and man-of-the-world. He had, too, the knack of getting on with anyone, in whatever walk of life.

Significantly enough, bearing in mind that the New Age of Aquarius began in the middle of the eighteenth century, Benjamin Franklin arrived on his first diplomatic mission to England on 27 July, 1757, to petition the King on behalf of the General Assembly of the State of Pennsylvania, against the proprietors of that state. His mission was successful. Subsequently, he came as agent for other states, and was a frequent visitor for long sojourns to both London and Paris. He made many friends with prominent and rising, political and intellectual stars of the period, including Mirabeau. His friendship with Mirabeau and other leaders of social reform in France undoubtedly influenced the course of events in that country.

The French Revolution would have happened anyway, but the American War of Independence was a very great encouragement and a stimulus to those in France who believed in Liberty, Equality and Fraternity. Benjamin Franklin was a man very much sought after in Paris and there is no doubt he played his part in bringing about the changes that took place in France, eight years after America won her independence.

Franklin most certainly did not approve of the ultimate violence and bloodshed that occurred during the Reign of Terror. The executions of Louis XIV, and later on, of Marie Antoinette – the guillotining not only of the flower of the French aristocracy, but thousands of other people as well – the orgy of blood-spilling by Robespierre and his followers, resulting in about 17,000 executions within the short period of fifteen months. All this would have been utterly abhorrent to Benjamin Franklin. He was very much against bloodshed in any form. Both Franklin and Mirabeau were moderates, and preferred to gain their objectives by reason rather than by force.

It is in character with the man that he was also president of an organisation devoted to the abolition of slavery. It was greatly due to his work that slavery was abolished in the northern states of America.

Although a busy diplomat, he, nevertheless, found time to make a very distinguished name for himself in the scientific world, and, as a result of his many researches and discoveries, he became a member of learned societies throughout Europe, and was honoured by the savants of numerous countries.

Franklin's considerable work in the electrical field brought him the Copley Medal of the Royal Society. His famous experiment with the kite, proving lightning was an electrical phenomenon was carried out in June, 1752. He conducted aeronautical experiments in France. He, also, made a very fine clock. A gentleman called Ferguson made an adaptation of it, and subsequently, introduced the clock to the general public.

It then became called Ferguson's Clock. Franklin, like Tesla a little more than a hundred years later, never bothered to patent many of his ideas. Consequently, others took the credit and benefited financially. He invented bifocal glasses which today are a source of comfortable sight to thousands of people, and, his work in the field of medicine caused him to be elected to the Royal Medical Society of Paris in 1777, and to become an Honorary Member of the Medical Society of London in 1787.

Franklin always hoped to be able to retire from public life and to spend the remainder of his days doing scientific research. His successes in this field during the time available makes one wonder what would have resulted if he had been able to give his whole life to it. An interesting conjecture.

There is no doubt that Benjamin Franklin was a genius. A most unusual man, brilliant in the diplomatic and political world, a scientist of no small stature, but above all, a man who helped to alter the course of history – by preserving and expanding the Renaissance begun in the days of Leonardo, and which was given a fresh direction in the Elizabethan era – and, ensured that this lamp of knowledge would burn more freely and even brighter, at the start of the Aquarian Age, *on both sides of the Atlantic.*

It was left to another genius – a veritable sun in human form – who was born sixty-six years after Franklin's death, to give the world a positive shower of scientific discoveries. Every man has his destiny to fulfil and Nikola Tesla, born in 1856, like Prometheus, literally gave the world light. His birthplace was at Smiljan, in the Austro-Hungarian border province of Lika. This is now a part of Yugoslavia.

In his boyhood, Tesla's thinking knew no bounds. Even then, he thought on a grand scale. John J. O'Neill describes how as a boy at school he was able to visualise the answers to problems – to see the whole sum, the components and the answer – in his mind, and he would astound his teachers with his quickness and his ability.[102] This faculty was to prove invaluable later on in life.

Even in those early schooldays, Tesla knew that he was different from his fellows. In his thoughts and boyhood activities he was the odd man out. He could do all the usual things that boys of his own age went in for, and, better too. His range of thought, however, was wider and not restricted. He liked to roam the countryside and his mind was already at work on the possibilities of harnessing the power in nature for the use of mankind.

Tesla was a brilliant scholar, who was equally fluent in eight languages, and was capable of working like so many unusually gifted men before him – Alexander the Great, Leonardo da Vinci and others – for abnormally long hours at a stretch, without sleep. However, Tesla, in his youth, on several occasions overdid this in his zest for knowledge, and suffered some serious ill-health, which brought him almost to the point of death itself.

Fortunately, for mankind, he recovered and was able, after some opposition, to follow his chosen profession, that of electrical engineering. Very early in life Tesla decided to devote his whole time to scientific research. He appears to have known from the very beginning of what he was capable, and that seems to have had no limitations. He had one main objective, to find out how this chemical world worked and to pass on his discoveries for the benefit of mankind. In order to accomplish that purpose he eliminated all distractions and embarked upon a life entirely devoted to single-pointed research in the electrical field.

Tesla had a fantastically retentive memory. He was a rapid reader and quite capable of remembering the contents of a whole page of a book, word perfect, years afterwards.

O'Neill relates that during Tesla's electrical engineering studies at the Polytechnic Institute, in Graz, Austria, the professor had demonstrated a direct current machine. The young Tesla, while appreciating its performance, had criticised the fact that a lot of sparking occurred at the commutator. Tesla suggested discarding the commutator and substituting alternating current. His professor told him in front of the class that this was impossible. Tesla was not really convinced and deep down inside he knew his idea was not only right, but possible.[103]

O'Neill gives us the sequel, and describes how Tesla was walking with his friend, Szigeti, one late afternoon in February, 1882, through a park in Budapest. There was a magnificent sunset to be seen as they strolled together. Tesla, as was often his habit, was reciting poetry. On this occasion he was speaking lines from Goethe's *Faust*. He was able to memorise volumes of classical works with comparative ease, and he knew the whole of *Faust* by heart, and could recite it without reference. The beautiful sunset reminded him of some of Goethe's lines.

> The glow retreats, done is the day of toil;
> It yonder hastes, new fields of life exploring;
> Ah, that no wing can lift me from the soil,
> Upon its track to follow, follow soaring . . .

It was after quoting these lines O'Neill tells us, that Tesla suddenly ejaculated 'Watch me reverse it!' His friend thought he was referring to the sun, and was naturally very concerned. What had happened was that Tesla's wonderful faculty for visualising objects had come into operation at that moment. The solution of alternating current had come to him then and there. He had seen the alternating current machine, complete and perfect in every detail. It had all been registered in his unusual mind.

Early in his career he came in contact with the perverse vagaries of human nature, especially with regard to money, and suffered from lack of capital to develop his beloved alternating current system. However, after a year of being forced, through having no other means of subsistence, to dig ditches as a labourer, Tesla eventually got backing to form a company.

From that time onward, discoveries in the electrical field poured from the creative mind of Tesla and astonished members of the electrical engineering profession, who recognised that a brilliant star had risen among them.

George Westinghouse, head of the Westinghouse Electric Company, became a close friend. He had the vision to see the great possibilities of Tesla's work and backed his alternating current motor against Edison's direct current system. The use of Tesla's alternating current system made it possible to harness the vast hydraulic power of Niagara Falls to produce electricity. This had been a boyhood dream of Tesla's.

The list of Tesla's scientific discoveries is too long to be covered completely here. Any one of them would have been the life work and achievement of an ordinary mortal, but Tesla was a man whose mind worked on all cylinders. He discovered the rotating magnetic field and the alternating current motor, the polyphase system of alternating currents and invented dynamos to generate them. He greatly improved the design and efficiency of Edison's direct current dynamos.

Another important invention was the robot or automaton, the forerunner of the 'electronic brain' we have today. This was a brilliant idea which developed the age of mechanisation and mass-production in industry.

Tesla too, discovered and worked with high-frequency currents, building oscillators for producing them.

He was using the principles of radar forty years before it was used in the Second World War. He operated a boat by remote control in 1898, and gave mankind what is now called radio. In 1890, he produced the first electronic tube for use as a detector in a radio system, and demonstrated it at lectures, both in London and Paris. His work in the radio field enabled him to propose a far-reaching, world-wide wireless system. Our present-day broadcasting system could be said to be but a smaller and somewhat different segment of Tesla's much greater concept, which included many other wonderful ideas still not in use.

Tesla frequently worked on several ideas at the same time. They often overlapped and developed from each other. In 1892, he demonstrated at a lecture lighted lamps which were without wire connections! These were also shown at the Chicago Columbian Exposition early in 1893, and he used them regularly in his own laboratory. He produced lamps, too, of far greater brilliance than those in use today, and they lasted almost indefinitely. Many of his discoveries which could have proved of great value and benefit to mankind were considered uncommercial and consequently, were not put on the market.

Tesla's work was on a colossal and cosmic scale. He thought and created at levels far above the human level. O'Neill relates how he devised a plan to transform the whole earth into one giant lamp, with the night sky completely illuminated. This would have enabled people to walk about out of doors at night without the use of street lighting, unless there was low cloud in the vicinity, and it would have been a tremendous aid to night navigation at sea.

He discovered, too, that power could be drawn from the earth anywhere, by making a connection with the ground, and filled the whole earth with electrical vibration by constructing a generator which spread artificial lightning. If this discovery had been taken up it would have been possible for anyone on payment of a small initial sum to install an antenna in their home, office or factory, and to have had permanent free electrical power without the use of wires. This would, however, have probably put the giant electrical combines almost out of business. Undoubtedly, this Tesla discovery which would have been of such world-wide benefit to humanity was, indeed, not commercial.

Time and again Tesla came up against financial set-backs. But these did not discourage him, and he persevered with his costly research. He was so busy that frequently he omitted to take out patents and his imitators took the credit, as well as the subsequent royalties. Tesla could have made millions. It is a tragedy in a sense that he did not do so, for the world would have had many more of his discoveries at its disposal today. However, although he liked to live well and was always well dressed, he was not extravagant and neither was he interested in money for its own sake. He was scrupulous in paying anyone who worked for him and was generous to an almost foolhardy degree.

Tesla always thought that he would live to be at least 150. Indeed, he hoped to continue with his research work until he reached the age of 100. He would then write his autobiography and put down on paper all his mentally held scientific notes for the benefit of posterity. However, fate or circumstances decided otherwise, and he died at the age of eighty-seven in 1943. At his death, although he had been a United States citizen for a very long time, all Tesla's records were sealed by the Custodian of Alien Property. No one was allowed by the American authorities to inspect these papers, except government officials.

The majority of the results of Tesla's scientific researches were not written down, but stored in his amazing memory. He kept his mind clear and unclouded by emotional reaction, and what is ordinarily called Visualisation was as real to him, and as durable, as any object in the chemical world. Therefore, he needed no extensive notebooks like those of Leonardo da Vinci. He could construct and test models of his inventions at this level.

Foreseeing the Second World War, Tesla offered the world an invention which he claimed would make war impossible. It would have made any country, of whatever size, safe inside its own frontiers. This wonderful offer was turned down.

Tesla, in his lifetime, did more than any other man to untie the mysterious knots of the chemical universe. His technological achievements have never been equalled. He was generous, not only with money when he had it (frequently he was without it and died almost impoverished), but with what he offered the world in the way of scientific discoveries. Often they were refused, but this did not deter him. Like other world teachers who preceded him, the teachings he offered were frequently rejected.

One day it will be realised that Tesla was a World Teacher for this Aquarian Age. The technology he gave to mankind brought about the biggest change in our way of life since the invention of the wheel thousands of years previously.

Through learning to understand and apply the technology that Tesla produced, mankind will be forced to work out a different and higher sense, both of values and ethics. This process has already begun and this time he has not been told exactly how to cope. It has not been handed to him on a silver platter. Man has been placed in a position where he has to work out the problem for himself. This, as a higher level of teaching, corresponds to the First Initiation of the Ancient Mystery Schools on a planetary scale.

Tesla has been called a superman, but is there really any such thing? He merely used the mind of Man creatively as it should be used. He gave the world light and power, and could have given much more if the world had been able to accept it.

18. Migrant or Marauder?

It's a pretty big area, you know, and all my investigations didn't touch more than the fringe of it. – *Rutherford*

We have seen in our story how the Atlanteans foresaw the sinking of Poseid, and how the wisest among them may have constructed the giant Temple of the Stars in Somerset, with its great zodiacal effigies, as a reminder to those who survived of their Atlantean heritage, and also of their connection with the people of the sky.

We have followed the fate of the remnant of humanity on earth after Poseid went down and the people wandered, trying to survive the catastrophic changes. We have suggested how earth man's heavenly counterpart, the Sky People, must have helped him undertake again the beginnings of a civilisation. We traced the first co-operation between the 'two brothers', one of whom was of the earth and the other from the sky, and have noted how that co-operative effort was made effective through a dual system of order and instruction.

We have gone along, in our imagination, with certain groups of people who fled and yet who somehow managed to remain together, taking with them from their lost home-land in the West the horse and knowledge of the wheel. These were the groups that remained isolated from the settled agricultural communities, leading a mobile life along the periphery of the new civilisation. They established themselves from Middle Europe far eastward into Russia along the rivers Danube, Dneiper, and Don. Their descendants became known as the Sons of Potei-Don, and they worshipped a Father God, the Lord Don – once the divine ruler of Atlantis. They brought his worship into Greece where he came to be called Poseidon. They, too, were in communication with the Sky People and received their share of advice and counsel during the Age of Gemini, and interpreted it in their own fashion according to their needs.

201

The Dual System persisted through the Age of Gemini (and a little longer). By the end of that age, the Sky People had begun to withdraw from active, open participation in the affairs of mankind. They had fostered, guided and taught him over a long period. Now it was to be up to earth man to fend for himself, since the human race had regained its vigour and its strength. However, before they left, the people of the sky gave mankind a parting present – The Great Pyramid – a veritable repository of knowledge for the future benefit of the human race.

Thus, not long after the New Age of Taurus (the Bull) began, the original Dual System ended. Menes united Upper and Lower Egypt into one kingdom, and the era of rulership under a single warrior king ensued. The Sky People had withdrawn, and the two existing systems of human culture, the agricultural and the more aggressive pastoral, began to merge – at the point of the sword. The warrior peoples came in from the periphery and overran the rich agricultural communities.

The Age of Taurus, like any other new zodiacal age, brought in sweeping changes, fresh ideas, and in this instance, the earliest recorded beginnings of technology. When the Sons of Poseidon thundered down with their horses and chariots into the relatively smaller, matriarchal farming areas, men took over the business of agriculture and industry was born. Mass-production of pottery, woven goods and other articles became possible.

On the religious side, the old Stone Age worship of the Mother Goddess declined or disappeared and was replaced by the veneration of a Father God. If the Mother Goddess remained, she was looked upon as his wife and assumed a secondary role.

Later, we considered the beginnings of Monotheism, the worship of one God, and traced the various stages of its development through the ideas of Abraham, Moses, Ezekiel, Jeremiah, Jesus and the Prophet Mahomet.

We looked on as the Sky People, very early in our tale, taught the people of Earth how to build the first round huts and hive-shaped houses, and we saw how, by the time of the first real settlements at Jarmo and Jericho, mankind was introduced to another dimension. His awareness and comprehension were moved on from the circle to the square, and we found him constructing rectangular buildings, able to confront a concept with its own image – as a wall duplicating and balancing another wall – and learning how to measure and discriminate.

These functions could be called the first beginnings of the art of Masonry since the sinking of Poseid, and the beginning of the long progress back to the standards of craftsmanship which produced the Gate of the Sun at Tiahuanaco and those enormous, perfect megalithic stones that form the substructure of the Temple of Baalbeck. Both of these examples of Atlantean architecture and building craft have survived untold thousands of years to bear witness in our own times to Antiquity.

The Temple of Jerusalem, planned by David and built by Solomon, marked a great step forward in the illumination of mankind, and celebrated his expanding achievements. In its modern form, the Craft of Freemasonry derives much of its symbolism from the building and later rebuilding of this Temple, and from details of its architecture. It is significant that the centre of Freemasonry is now in England, and that the formation of the first Grand Lodge was but a few years before the true beginning of the Aquarian Age in the middle of the eighteenth century.

In every zodiacal age there are peak periods of activity a century or so before the end of that age. These are prophetic times and are years of serious preparation for the coming New Age. The sixth century BC, towards the end of the Age of Aries, was no exception to this rule, and in its effect compares amazingly with its counterpart near the end of the Piscean Age, the sixteenth century AD.

The sixth century BC produced a galaxy of new ideas. Lao Tze, Confucius and Buddha, in the eastern part of the world, taught of the enormous possibilities latent in mankind. Amos and Jeremiah, farther to the west, preached of an international and indeed universal God. If these two main streams of thought could have been brought together, what course would the history of mankind have taken? What would have been the effect upon the development of civilisation? And to what ethical and moral heights would humanity have risen by this time? These are all questions that occupy the minds of many thinkers and philosophers in our own era, and in this age of communication the two sets of concepts are beginning to be evaluated as complementary systems of philosophy.

The new Age of Pisces began with violence and revolution, as did the following Age of Aquarius. Alexander, the god-king, blazed his trail across the Orient, achieving his task of uniting the many small and squabbling countries and city states into one unit, under one ruler – himself. This was his part to play in the general influence of expanding ideas and broadening activities opening up the New Age. Although his enormous empire did not survive him and was divided up, the resulting divisions were greater than the original units out of which Alexander had forged the whole.

Alexander was followed by Jesus, another revolutionary of a different order, the Nazarene who broke away from the established faith of his time.

The Age of the Fishes, then, rushed upon the world in a torrent of unrest. Nearly everyone came into contact with new ideas and extraordinary concepts, and often the new had to break through the old order with violence. Euripides, Sophocles and Socrates all died within a few years of one another during the last decade of the Age of Aries, the Ram. Aristophanes and Plato brought their influences into the beginning of the Piscean Age, but the year after the death of Alexander saw the deaths, also, of Aristotle and Demosthenes. The greatest names in the next century are those of Euclid and Archimedes. Athens was allied with Rome, and Hannibal crossed the Alps. The world had more than two centuries still to wait before the coming of Jesus of Nazareth, but the waiting was never quiet. The ferment at every level continued and spread. Horace, Ovid, Livy and Virgil were all living in the last century BC. The last of these, Virgil, did not die until AD 19. The world had received the framework of ideas upon which the New Age would be built.

Only after all this had been accomplished did the world receive the spiritual message of the age. Unless this Aquarian Age of ours is following a different pattern, we still have about two more centuries to wait for the great revelation pertaining to the era. We are living, now, in the very middle of the period preceding it, the time of unrest, of reorganisation and readjustment on every level of mundane affairs.

During much of the remainder of the Age of Pisces until the sixteenth century, which compares in its effects to the sixth century BC, the search for knowledge pertaining to this world was not freely cultivated. These times we now call the Dark Ages. The lamps of learning were kept alight by the sons of Islam, and later the wicks were renewed by the Renaissance, to give more light.

The sixteenth century, the era of the Elizabethans, expanded and developed the contributions of the Renaissance, and spread its influence throughout the known and unknown world. Elizabeth, by her brilliant statecraft, thwarted both Philip of Spain and Rome, and the light of the Renaissance continued to expand. That century, like the sixth century BC, was one overflowing with new ideas. It was an astounding age filled with brilliant and outstanding men: William Shakespeare, Francis Bacon, Walter Ralegh, Philip Sidney, Edmund Spenser and Christopher Marlowe. All contributed magnificently to the Elizabethan era, as did many other men whose greatness varied with their individual talents. These were men like Martin Frobisher, Humphrey Gilbert, and Sir Francis Drake; William Cecil and Sir Francis Walsingham. They were not merely superb seamen and great statesmen: they were Elizabethans. They were essentially individualists, but at the same time there was something that bound them together in a fraternity of action – an ability to create and to accept change.

The Renaissance and the Elizabethan era were preparatory steps toward the Aquarian Age, which began in the middle of the eighteenth century. This New Age, too, was ushered in with violence, revolutions, and a flood of new ideas and concepts, just as the age which preceded it had been, the Age of Pisces. Soon after its inception there came the American War of Independence (1775-1784), followed by the French Revolution (1789-1794), and these two events set the political and social development of mankind upon a new course unparalleled in history.

New discoveries and developments in astronomy, technology, and social thinking poured in upon the civilised world in an ever increasing cascade. The planet Uranus was discovered in 1781. The first successful steam engine appeared in 1825. Slavery was abolished in the British Colonies in 1833. A year later Faraday discovered the phenomenon of self-induction, and in 1846 the planet Neptune was found.

Only ten years later, Nikola Tesla was born. The impetus that Tesla gave the world is still not fully appreciated. His one-pointed aim was to find out how the chemical world worked and to pass on his innumerable discoveries to humanity. The world did not accept everything he offered, which seems too bad. Imitators appeared and took the credit for many of his discoveries. This did not worry him unduly. He knew no jealousy. He never disparaged the achievements of his contemporaries, and he was always ready to give praise and recognition when and where it was due.

Tesla was not really interested in obtaining the material things of this world. His first consideration was pure research. At one time, in order to help his friend George Westinghouse and to enable the Westinghouse Electric Company to continue to back his alternating current motor, he tore up a contract worth to him 12,000,000 dollars in royalties.[104] This has been acclaimed as a great sacrifice on Tesla's part. It was nothing of the sort. At that time he was a rich man, anyway. His action was motivated by an altruism outside and beyond the personal scope of sacrifice, at a level and in dimensions where mere royalties had no real value. Above all, he wanted the world to have the use of the principle of alternating current, and the only way to enable the company to continue to promote it was for him to forgo the remainder of the contract.

We have already discussed the myriads of technical inventions that the great Tesla gave the world as the manifold result of his discoveries. The material benefits derived from them and the host of new concepts they have made possible have broadened our horizons so much that we are now ready to reach up into Outer Space.

Tesla's death in 1943 brings us almost up to present time. We have come a long way, and this book has simply been another look at history. However, it is hoped that this book differs from other historical surveys in at least two ways.

They are related to one another, and yet are different. Their importance lies not so much in their form as in their function, and they are: the scope (the horizons) of the view taken, and the angle from which the historical and prehistorical landscape is contemplated (the point of view).

Mankind in the Air Age of Aquarius has already asserted his dominion over the kingdom of the Air in both the fields of Communication and of Transport. He is busily teaching himself to control other atmospheric phenomena. Already he is reaching out beyond his atmosphere into the vast ocean of Space, which is the esoteric or hidden meaning of the Aquarian Symbol. The water poured out (controlled) by the Water Man is no earthly fluid, but is, in reality, that cosmic element we know as Space. God willing, before the end of this age, mankind will have won the freedom of this expanded and expansive environment. He has already taken his first steps in that direction and, in so doing, has added a third dimension to his universe.

The Earth was flat to Man until voyagers upon its apparently endless seas proved it to be a mighty sphere. Even after the invention and development of telescopic instruments, the sky remained a flattened canopy (or an even flatter photographic print) to earth man, as far as his own personal reality concerning it could go. Now that he is beginning to venture out upon this greater ocean, and as he listens to the electronic voices of the probes he sends out farther than he, himself, can go, the reality of this third dimension outward is growing stronger. Much the same sort of thing that happened to the mind of Man when the attitudes of the old Stone Age gave way before new concepts of the air and sky is happening again. This time, however, it is taking place upon a wider turn of the geometric spiral of mankind's increasingly rapid progress and evolution.

The proof that the Earth is a sphere was, in a sense, a Stone Age fulfilment. It brought mankind a better understanding of his Great Mother, the planet upon which he dwells.

On the other hand, his exploration of Space has forced him to raise his eyes and to look upward and outward into the Universe that is, in fact, his true home. Again, the effect of this necessary reorientation is much the same as the change that came over the minds of people in the city cultures who had largely inherited the religious attitudes of their Stone Age forefathers, when the Sons of Potei-Don brought them the ancient Atlantean worship of the God of the Sky. In our own times the effect is more intense and therefore more powerful.

Mankind no longer looks to his Mother Earth for the fulfilment of all his needs. He has explored her inward three dimensions and his own, not completely as yet, but well enough to become aware of other needs and other desires. He has found himself to be mobile, and he is on the move. Where he will go in the chemical universe is limited only by his ability to solve its problems, and that ability is very great, indeed.

Now, like the people who took part in the great migrations that began the real civilisation of the world, mankind is moving out away from his old homeland – the Mother Planet, Earth. If he is to survive this greatest of all fold-wanderings, he must learn how to take his mind along with him, for if he does not learn to expand the horizons of his thinking in both space and time he will go out as an uncomprehending savage. If that should happen, the result can only spell disaster for him and for whatever he meets on the way, whether it be living and intelligent or merely material.

Earlier in this book, we have described the Temple of the Stars in Somerset, and we said that it was intended to keep alive the recollection of a purpose, a promise and a prophecy. The purpose was to maintain a link between the two brother races, the one of earth and the other from beyond it, and we have seen in our story how some of that purpose has been carried out.

The promise that the two separated brother groups will, in time, come together again for their mutual benefit has not yet been openly fulfilled, but the numerous sightings all over the world in recent years – modern visions of celestial chariots – may well foreshadow such an event.

The prophecy was reiterated by the Nazarene nearly 2,000 years ago, and points to this age in which we are now privileged to be living, the Age of Aquarius – the Age of Space.

A Note on the Chalice Well at Glastonbury

by Major W. Tudor Pole, O.B.E.

At the beginning of 1959 it was my privilege to launch a wonderful adventure. The Chalice Well estate at Glastonbury, Somerset, lies on the slopes of Chalice Hill, almost under the shadow of the far-famed Micael Tor.

With the co-operation of a group of friends, the property has now been vested in a charitable trust and the hallowed well, the gardens and Little St Michael Hostel are now open to all comers, irrespective of race, class or creed.

The story has already been told in many books and pamphlets readily available to all who are interested in Celtic Christianity and the arrival of Christ's Message in Britain within fifty years of the Crucifixion.

Joseph of Arimathea is believed to have brought with him the Cup used at the Last Supper and to have buried it for safe keeping beneath Chalice Hill within a stone's throw of the well itself. I believe that the Cup or Chalice is destined to become the symbol for the new age now dawning, and it is my hope that Chalice Well may once more fulfil the inspiring mission of acting as a gateway through which revelation for coming times may flow, radiating from there across Britain and the world.

It is my conviction that the people of our island will be given the opportunity once more to lead humanity out of the present darkness into the Light.

I firmly believe that it lies within the capacity of our children to carry out this task. In my view the discerning among them should lose no time in preparing themselves to fulfil a Destiny that most surely will be presented to them and at no very distant date.

(Readers who are interested can obtain further information from the Custodian, Chalice Wells Trust, Little St Michael, Glastonbury, Somerset.)

Reference Notes

1. *The View over Atlantis*, by John Michell, p. 17.
2. *The Great Pyramid, its divine message*, by D. Davidson and H. Aldersmith, p. 239.
3. *The Bible as History*, by Dr Werner Keller, pp. 48-50.
4. *A History of Architecture*, by Sir Banister Fletcher, 16th edition, reprinted 1959, p. 933.
5. Ibid., p. 932.
6. *The Growth of Civilisation*, by W. J. Perry, Chapter 5.
7. *Built Before the Flood*, by H. S. Bellamy.
8. *Earth in Upheaval*, by Immanuel Velikovsky, p. 70.
9. An article by Alexandre Kazantsev, in *Le Courrier Interplanetaire*, September 1961 issue, reproduced from *Komsomolskaia Pravda*, of 14 May, 1961.
10. *Mysteries of Ancient South America*, by Harold T. Wilkins, p. 19.
11. *Aku-Aku*, by Thor Heyerdahl.
12. *A History of Architecture*, by Sir Banister Fletcher, 16th edition, reprinted 1969, p. 153.
13. *A Handbook and Atlas of Astronomy*, by W. Peck, F.R.A.S., pp. 1-10.
14. *A Guide to Glastonbury's Temple of the Stars*, by K. E. Maltwood (revised edition, 1950).
15. Ibid., p. 1.
16. Ibid., p. 5.
17. Ibid., p. 11.
18. Ibid., p. 128.
19. *Guardian of the Grail*, by John Whitehead.
20. *The Sky People*, by Brinsley le Poer Trench, pp. 31-52.
21. *A Guide to Glastonbury's Temple of the Stars*, by K. E. Maltwood (revised edition, 1950), p. 94.
22. Ibid., p. 94. K. E. Maltwood's reference to the Welsh Bard comes from *The Mythology and Rites of the British Druids*, by Edward Davis (J. Booth, 1809).
23. Ibid., p. 95.
24. *Guardian of the Grail*, by John Whitehead, Glossary, p. 290.
25. Ibid., p. 224.
26. Ibid., pp. 15 and 16.

27. *The Secret Doctrine*, by Madame H. P. Blavatsky (third and revised edition), Vol. 1, p. 248.
28. Ibid., Vol. 2, p. 577.
29. *Studies in Symbolism*, by Marguerite Mertens-Steinon, p. 63.
30. Ibid., p. 63.
31. Ibid., p. 47.
32. Ibid., p. 48.
33. Ibid., p. 44.
34. *A Guide to Glastonbury's Temple of the Stars*, by K. E. Maltwood (revised edition, 1950), p. 5, quoting from Didot edition of Plutarch, Vol. 3, p. 511.
35. *The Encircled Serpent*, by M. Oldfield Howey, p. 103.
36. *Guardian of the Grail*, by John Whitehead, pp. 68 and 69.
37. *The Old Straight Track*, by Alfred Watkins.
38. *The View over Atlantis*, by John Michell, pp. 47-50.
39. *Stonehenge Decoded*, by Professor G. S. Hawkins.
40. *Immortal Britain*, by Alan V. Insole, p. 80.
41. *The Secret Doctrine*, by Madame H. P. Blavatsky (third and revised edition), Vol. 1, pp. 237 and 238.
42. *Abury, a Temple of the British Druids*, by the Rev. William Stukeley, M.D.
43. *The Encircled Serpent*, by M. Oldfield Howey, pp. 2 and 3.
44. Ibid., p. 11.
45. *Men, God and Magic*, by Ivar Lissnar, p. 165.
46. *White Horses and Other Hill Figures*, by Morris Marples, p. 46.
47. *Immortal Britain*, by Alan V. Insole, p. 74.
48. Ibid., p. 74.
49. Ibid., p. 74.
50. Ibid., p. 75.
51. Ibid., p. 75.
52. *The Growth of Civilisation*, by W. J. Perry, Chapter 5.
53. *The Hittites*, by O. R. Gurney, p. 184.
54. *Myth and Symbol in Ancient Egypt*, by R. T. Rundle Clark, p. 97.
55. Ibid., p. 98.
56. Ibid., p. 103.
57. Ibid., p. 21.
58. *The Secret Doctrine*, by Madame H. P. Blavatsky (third and revised edition), Vol. 2, p. 793. Madame Blavatsky is quoting from M. Joly's *Man before Metals*, p. 184.
60. *The Pyramids of Egypt*, by I. E. S. Edwards, p. 2.
61. *The Great Pyramid, its divine message*, by D. Davidson and H. Aldersmith, p. 213.

62. Isaiah xix, 19.
63. *The Bible as History*, by Dr Werner Keller, pp. 119 and 120.
64. *The Lost Pharaohs*, by Leonard Cottrell, p. 77.
65. *The Shadow of Atlantis*, by Colonel A. Braghine, p. 49.
66. *The Great Pyramid, its divine message*, by D. Davidson and H. Aldersmith, p. 77.
67. Ibid., p. 11.
68. *The Growth of Civilisation*, by W. J. Perry, Chapter 7.
69. Ibid., Chapter 7.
70. *Itinerary of 'The Somerset Giants'*, abridged from *King Arthur's Round Table of the Zodiac*, by K. E. Maltwood, pp. 12 and 13.
71. *The Secret Doctrine* (third and revised edition), Vol. 2, pp. 371-372.
72. *The Twelve Olympians*, by Charles Seltman, p. 144.
73. Ibid., p. 144.
74. *A Forgotten Kingdom*, by Sir Leonard Woolley, p. 192.
75. *Larousse Encyclopaedia of Mythology*, p. 219.
76. *From the Tablets of Sumer*, by Dr Samuel Noah Kramer.
77. Ibid., p. 241.
78. Ibid., p. 231.
79. Ibid., p. 27.
80. *History and Monuments of Ur*, by C. J. Gadd, p. 85.
81. *From the Tablets of Sumer*, by Dr Samuel Noah Kramer, p. 269.
82. *The Encyclopaedia Britannica*, 11th edition, Vol. 13, p. 178.
83. Genesis iii, 6.
84. Ibid., iv, 20.
85. John i, 6.
86. I Samuel, xvi, 1.
87. Ibid., xvi, 11 and 12.
88. I Chronicles, Chapters xxi and xxii.
89. *The Bible as History*, by Dr Werner Keller, p. 67.
90. I Chronicles, Chapter xxi.
91. Ibid., xxviii, 12.
92. I Kings iv, 34.
93. Ibid., vii, 14.
94. II Chronicles ii, 13.
95. Ibid., ii, 14.
96. *The Encyclopaedia Britannica*, 11th edition, Vol. 23, p. 84.
97. Ibid., Vol. 26, p. 722.
98. *The Sky People*, by Brinsley le Poer Trench, p. 42.
99. *The Encyclopaedia Britannica*, 11th edition, Vol. 3. p. 499.
100. Ibid., Vol. 16, p. 450.

101. *The Tudors*, by Christopher Morris, p. 185, quoting from *Venetian Calendar*, VIII, p. 344.
102. *Prodigal Genius, the life of Nikola Tesla*, by John J. O'Neill, p. 23.
103. Ibid., pp. 40-42.
104. Ibid., pp. 80-82.

Further Reading

The Bible.

The Koran.

The Encyclopaedia Britannica, 11th edition.

The Concise Encyclopaedia of Archaeology, edited by Leonard Cottrell. Hutchinson & Co., London, 1960.

A History of Architecture, by Sir Banister Fletcher. B. T. Batsford Ltd., London, 16th edition, reprinted 1959.

A Handbook and Atlas of Astronomy, by W. Peck, F.R.A.S. Gall and Inglis, London, 1890.

Earth in Upheaval, by Immanuel Velikovsky. Victor Gollancz Ltd., in association with Sidgwick & Jackson Ltd., London, 1956.

Built before the Flood, by H. S. Bellamy. Faber and Faber, London, 1943.

The Encircled Serpent, by M. Oldfield Howey. Arthur Richmond Company, New York, 1955.

Aku-Aku, by Thor Heyerdahl. Penguin Books, Harmondsworth, Middlesex, England, 1960.

The Shadow of Atlantis, by Colonel A. Braghine. Rider & Co., London, 1938.

The Stars in our Heavens, Myths and Fables, by Peter Lunn. Thames and Hudson, London, 1951.

The Ancient Myths, by Norman Lorre Goodrich. The New American Library of World Literature, Inc., New York, 1960.

The Myths of Greece and Rome, by H. A. Guerber. George G. Harrap & Co., Ltd., London, 1907.

The Secret Doctrine, by Madame H. P. Blavatsky. Third revised edition, Theosophical Publishing House, London, 1928.

Studies in Symbolism, by Marguerite Mertens-Steinon. Theosophical Publishing House, London, 1933.

Men, God and Magic, by Ivar Lissnar. Jonathan Cape, London, 1961.

The Bible as History, by Dr Werner Keller, Hodder & Stoughton, London, 1956.

Immortal Britain, by Alan V. Insole. The Aquarian Press, London, 1952.

White Horses and Other Hill Figures, by Morris Marples. Country Life Ltd., London, 1949.

Abury, A Temple of the British Druids, by the Rev. William Stukeley, M.D., London, 1743.

Stonehenge, by R. J. C. Atkinson. Hamish Hamilton, London, 1956.

The Riddle of Prehistoric Britain, by Comyns Beaumont. Rider & Co., London, 1945.

A Guide to Prehistoric Britain, by Nicholas Thomas. B. T. Batsford Ltd., London, 1960.

A Guide to Glastonbury's Temple of the Stars, by K. E. Maltwood. John Watkins, 21, Cecil Court, Charing Cross Road, London, 1934.

Itinerary of 'The Somerset Giants', abridged from *King Arthur's Round Table of the Zodiac*, by K. E. Maltwood. Victoria Printing & Publishing Co., Victoria, Canada, 1946.

The Children of the Sun, by W. J. Perry. Methuen & Co., London, 1923.

The Growth of Civilisation, by W. J. Perry. Methuen & Co., London, 1924.

Mysteries of Ancient South America, by Harold T. Wilkins. Rider & Co., London, 1946.

Alexander, the God, by Maurice Druon. Rupert Hart-Davis, London, 1960.

The Hittites, by O. R. Gurney. Penguin Books, Harmondsworth, Middlesex, England, 1952.

The Bull of Minos, by Leonard Cottrell. Evans Brothers Ltd., London, 1953.

The Gods of Prehistoric Man, by J. Maringer. Weidenfeld & Nicolson, London, 1960.

The Twelve Olympians, by Charles Seltman. Pan Books, London, 1952.

A Forgotten Kingdom, by Sir Leonard Woolley. Penguin Books Ltd., Harmondsworth, Middlesex, England, 1953.

It Began in Babel, by Herbert Wendt. Weidenfeld & Nicolson, London, 1958.

From the Tablets of Sumer, by Dr Samuel Noah Kramer. The Falcon's Wing Press, Indian Hills, Colorado, 1956.

Myth and Symbol in Ancient Egypt, by R. T. Rundle Clark. Thames and Hudson, London, 1959.

The Pyramids of Egypt, by I. E. S. Edwards. Max Parrish, London, 1961.

The Great Pyramid, its divine message, by D. Davidson and H. Aldersmith. Williams & Norgate, London, 1929.

The Lost Pharaohs, by Leonard Cottrell. Pan Books Ltd., London, 1956.

Guardian of the Grail, by John Whitehead. Jarrolds, London, 1959.

The Arthurian Legend, by Margaret J. C. Reid. Oliver & Boyd, London, 1938.

King Arthur's Avalon, by Geoffrey Ashe. Collins, London, 1957, and Fontana, London, 1973.

Morte D'Arthur, by Sir Thomas Malory, Everyman's Library, London, 1919.

The Romance of Leonardo da Vinci, by Dmitri Merejcovski. The Heritage Press, New York, 1938.

Elizabeth the Great, by Elizabeth Jenkins. Victor Gollancz Ltd., London, 1959.

Queen Elizabeth I, by J. E. Neale. Jonathan Cape, London, 1934.

Prodigal Genius, the Life of Nikola Tesla, by John J. O'Neill. Ives Washburn Inc., New York, 1944.

The Tudors, by Christopher Morris. B. T. Batsford Ltd., London, 1955 and Fontana, London, 1966.

Archaic Egypt, by W. B. Emery. Penguin Books, Harmondsworth, Middlesex, England, 1961.

Larousse Encyclopaedia of Mythology, Batchworth Press, London, 1959.

History and Monuments of Ur, by C. J. Gadd. Chatto & Windus, London, 1929.

Prehistoric Britain, by Jacquetta and Christopher Hawkes. Penguin Books, Harmondsworth, Middlesex, England, 1944.

Mysterious Britain, by Janet and Colin Bord. Garnstone Press, London, 1972.

The Flying Saucer Vision, by John Michell. Sidgwick and Jackson, London, 1967.

The View over Atlantis, by John Michell. Garnstone Press, London, 1969.

Stonehenge Decoded, by Professor G. S. Hawkins. Souvenir Press, London, 1966.

The Old Straight Track, by Alfred Watkins. Methuen & Co., London, 1966.

The Quest for Arthur's Britain, edited by Geoffrey Ashe. Pall Mall Press, London, 1968, and Paladin, London, 1971.

The Ley Hunter Magazine. Edited by Paul Screeton, 5 Egton Drive, Seaton Carew, Hartlepool, Co. Durham.

Index

far away places . . . visitors from other worlds . . .
the wonders of ancient civilizations . . .
the ancestors of Man . . .

from **Ballantine**

ANCIENT ENGINEERS, by L. Sprague de Camp.
From the pyramids of Egypt and the Great Wall of China to the "no parking" signs at Nineveh and the water alarm clock of Plato.
From the author of **Citadels of Mystery**   **$1.75**
As fascinating as Chariot of the Gods

TEMPLE OF THE STARS, by Brinsley le Poer Trench.
An examination of Mankind's ancient link with visitors from distant stars as seen in astrological theories.
By the former editor of **Flying Saucer Review**   **$1.50**

PILTDOWN MEN, by Ronald Millar.
Here is the story, as fascinating as a whodunit, of how the Piltdown skull came to be discovered; how the hoax was exposed; and who the hoaxer may have been.   **$1.75**

IN SEARCH OF THE MAYA, by Robert L. Brunhouse.
The wonder, the disbelief, the unfolding of the idea of a unique culture as sophisticated as that of the Old World was a genuine discovery and as fascinating an adventure as any that can be found in exploration or archeology.   **$1.65**